Principles in Practice

The Principles in Practice imprint offers teachers concrete illustrations of effective classroom practices based in NCTE research briefs and policy statements. Each book discusses the research on a specific topic, links the research to an NCTE brief or policy statement, and then demonstrates how those principles come alive in practice: by showcasing actual classroom practices that demonstrate the policies in action; by talking about research in practical, teacher-friendly language; and by offering teachers possibilities for rethinking their own practices in light of the ideas presented in the books. Books within the imprint are grouped in strands, each strand focused on a significant topic of interest.

Adolescent Literacy Strand

Adolescent Literacy at Risk? The Impact of Standards (2009) Rebecca Bowers Sipe

Adolescents and Digital Literacies: Learning Alongside Our Students (2010) Sara Kajder

Adolescent Literacy and the Teaching of Reading: Lessons for Teachers of Literature (2010) Deborah Appleman

Rethinking the "Adolescent" in Adolescent Literacy (2017) Sophia Tatiana Sarigianides, Robert Petrone, and Mark A. Lewis

Restorative Justice in the English Language Arts Classroom (2019) Maisha T. Winn, Hannah Graham, and Rita Renjitham Alfred

Writing in Today's Classrooms Strand

Writing in the Dialogical Classroom: Students and Teachers Responding to the Texts of Their Lives (2011) Bob Fecho

Becoming Writers in the Elementary Classroom: Visions and Decisions (2011) Katie Van Sluys

Writing Instruction in the Culturally Relevant Classroom (2011) Maisha T. Winn and Latrise P. Johnson

Writing Can Change Everything: Middle Level Kids Writing Themselves into the World (2020) Shelbie Witte, editor

Literacy Assessment Strand

Our Better Judgment: Teacher Leadership for Writing Assessment (2012) Chris W. Gallagher and Eric D. Turley

Beyond Standardized Truth: Improving Teaching and Learning through Inquiry-Based Reading Assessment (2012) Scott Filkins

Reading Assessment: Artful Teachers, Successful Students (2013) Diane Stephens, editor

Going Public with Assessment: A Community Practice Approach (2018) Kathryn Mitchell Pierce and Rosario Ordoñez-Jasis

Literacies of the Disciplines Strand

Entering the Conversations: Practicing Literacy in the Disciplines (2014) Patricia Lambert Stock, Trace Schillinger, and Andrew Stock

Real-World Literacies: Disciplinary Teaching in the High School Classroom (2014) Heather Lattimer

Doing and Making Authentic Literacies (2014) Linda Denstaedt, Laura Jane Roop, and Stephen Best

Reading in Today's Classrooms Strand

Connected Reading: Teaching Adolescent Readers in a Digital World (2015) Kristen Hawley Turner and Troy Hicks

Digital Reading: What's Essential in Grades 3–8 (2015) William L. Bass II and Franki Sibberson

Teaching Reading with YA Literature: Complex Texts, Complex Lives (2016) Jennifer Buehler

Teaching English Language Learners Strand

Beyond "Teaching to the Test": Rethinking Accountability and Assessment for English Language Learners (2017) Betsy Gilliland and Shannon Pella

Community Literacies en Confianza: *Learning from Bilingual After-School Programs* (2017) Steven Alvarez

Understanding Language: Supporting ELL Students in Responsive ELA Classrooms (2017) Melinda J. McBee Orzulak

Writing across Culture and Language: Inclusive Strategies for Working with ELL Writers in the ELA Classroom (2017) Christina Ortmeier-Hooper

Students' Rights to Read and Write Strand

Adventurous Thinking: Fostering Students' Rights to Read and Write in Secondary ELA Classrooms (2019) Mollie V. Blackburn, editor

Writing Can Change Everything

Middle Level Kids Writing Themselves into the World

Edited by

Shelbie Witte
Oklahoma State University

National Council of Teachers of English
340 N. Neil St., Suite #104, Champaign, Illinois 61820
www.ncte.org

Staff Editor: Bonny Graham
Imprint Editor: Cathy Fleischer
Interior Design: Victoria Pohlmann
Cover Design: Pat Mayer
Cover Image: Marvin Young

NCTE Stock Number: 74876; eStock Number: 74883
ISBN 978-0-8141-7487-6; eISBN 978-0-8141-7488-3

Library of Congress Cataloging-in-Publication Data
Names: Witte, Shelbie, editor.
Title: Writing can change everything : middle level kids writing themselves into the world / edited by Shelbie Witte.
Description: Champaign, Illinois : National Council of Teachers of English, 2020. | Includes bibliographical references and index. | Summary: "Seven teacher-writers share their approaches to mentoring, modeling, and facilitating middle level writers to explore their places in the world, grounding their work in NCTE's Professional Knowledge for the Teaching of Writing position statement"—Provided by publisher.
Identifiers: LCCN 2020005063 (print) | LCCN 2020005064 (ebook) | ISBN 9780814174876 (trade paperback) | ISBN 9780814174883 (adobe pdf)
Subjects: LCSH: Composition (Language arts)—Study and teaching (Middle school) | English language—Composition and exercises—Study and teaching (Middle school)
Classification: LCC LB1631 .W725 2020 (print) | LCC LB1631 (ebook) | DDC 372.623—dc23
LC record available at https://lccn.loc.gov/2020005063
LC ebook record available at https://lccn.loc.gov/2020005064

To the beautiful dissonance of middle level kids and the teachers
who love them

Contents

Professional Knowledge for the Teaching of Writing

Approved in February 2016, this revised statement replaces the *NCTE Beliefs about the Teaching of Writing* (November 2004), now sunsetted.

A subcommittee of the NCTE Executive Committee wrote the *NCTE Beliefs about the Teaching of Writing* in 2004. In over a decade since, the everyday experience of writing in people's lives has expanded dramatically. Increasingly, handheld devices are important instruments for people's writing, integrated tightly, nearly seamlessly, with their composing in video, photographs, and other media. Geographic location and embodied presence have become more salient to writing than at most times in human history. The ways writing and the spoken voice are mutually supportive in writing processes have become increasingly facilitated by technological capabilities. Globalized economies and relative ease of transportation have continued to bring languages into contact with one another, and US educational scholars and, sometimes, institutions have made progress in considering what it means for individuals to be adding new written languages to existing ones. Even as these expansions have enlarged the experience of writing outside school, implementation of the first USA nationwide standards in literacy—the Common Core State Standards—has, in some places, contributed to narrowing students' experience of writing inside school. In that contradictory and shifting environment, the NCTE Executive Committee charged a committee to update the *Beliefs about the Teaching of Writing*, attempting to reflect some of the historically significant changes of recent years. What follows are some of the professional principles that guide effective teaching.

Writing grows out of many purposes

Writing is not just one practice or activity. A note to a cousin is not like a business report, which is different again from a poem. The processes and ways of thinking that lead to these varied kinds of texts can also vary widely, from the quick email to a friend to the careful drafting and redrafting of a legal contract. The different purposes and genres both grow out of and create varied relationships between the writers and the readers, and existing relationships are reflected in degrees of formality in language, as well as assumptions about what knowledge and experience are already shared, and what needs to be explained. Writing with certain purposes in mind, the writer focuses attention on what the audience is thinking or believing; other times, the writer focuses more on the information she or he is organizing, or on her or his own emergent thoughts and feelings. Therefore, the thinking, procedures, and physical format in writing are shaped in accord with the author's purpose(s), the needs of the audience, and the conventions of the genre.

Often, in school, students write only to prove that they did something they were asked to do, in order to get credit for it. Or, students are taught a single type of writing and are led to believe this type will suffice in all situations. Since writers outside school have many different purposes beyond demonstrating accountability and they use more diverse genres

Professional Knowledge for the Teaching of Writing

of writing, it is important that students have experiences within school that teach them how writing differs with purpose, audience, and other elements of the situation. Even within more academic settings like college courses, the characteristics of good writing vary among disciplines; what counts as a successful lab report, for example, differs from a successful history paper, online discussion contribution, essay exam, reflection on service learning, or interpretative statement about a work of art.

Thus, beyond the traditional purposes that are identified in school, purposes for writing include developing social networks; reasoning with others to improve society; supporting personal and spiritual growth; reflecting on experience; communicating professionally and academically; building relationships with others, including friends, family, and like-minded individuals; and engaging in aesthetic experiences.

What does this mean for teaching?

In order to provide high-quality writing opportunities for all students, teachers need to understand

- The wide range of purposes for which people write and the different kinds of texts and processes that arise from those purposes;
- Strategies and forms for writing for public participation in a democratic society;
- Ways people use writing for personal growth, expression, and reflection, and how to encourage and develop this kind of writing;
- How people make creative and literary texts, aesthetic genres, for the purposes of entertainment, pleasure, or exploration;
- The ways digital environments have added new modalities while constantly creating new publics, audiences, purposes, and invitations to compose;
- The range of non-public uses of writing for self-organization, reflection, planning, and management of information, and the many tools, digital and otherwise, that people use for these purposes;
- Appropriate genres for varied academic disciplines and the purposes and relationships that create those forms;
- Ways of organizing and transforming school curricula in order to provide students with adequate education in varied purposes for writing;
- How to set up a course that asks students to write for varied purposes and audiences.

Related:

Writing Now: A Policy Research Brief Produced by the National Council of Teachers of English [1]

Writing is embedded in complex social relationships and their appropriate languages

Writing happens in the midst of a web of relationships. Most clearly, the relationship between the writer and the reader can be very specific: writers often have a definite idea of who will read their work, not just a generalized notion that their text will be available to the world. Furthermore, particular people surround the writer—other writers, friends, members

Professional Knowledge for the Teaching of Writing

of a given community—during the process of composing. They may know what the writer is doing and be indirectly involved in it, though they are not the audience for the work. In workplace and academic settings, writers often write because someone in authority tells them to. Therefore, power relationships are built into the writing situation. In every writing situation, the writer, the reader, and all relevant others live in a structured social order, where some people's words count more than others, where being heard is more difficult for some people than others, where some people's words come true and others' do not.

Writers start in different places. It makes a difference what kinds of language writers spoke while growing up and may speak at home now, and how those experiences relate to the kinds of language they are being asked to take when composing. It makes a difference, too, the culture a writer comes from, the ways people use language in that culture and the degree to which that culture is privileged in the larger society. Important cultural differences are not only linguistic but also racial, economic, geographic, and ideological. Digital environments have created new contexts in which new languages are being invented continuously, and young people are often leading innovators of "digitalk." The Internet brings global languages into contact, even as it provides new contexts for each language—written and oral—to change.

What does this mean for teaching?

The teaching of writing should assume students will begin with the language with which they are most at home and most fluent in their speech. That language may be a variety of English or a different language altogether. The languages students learn first are the bedrock upon which all other language traditions and forms will be constructed. The ultimate goal is not to leave students where they are, however, but to move them toward greater flexibility, so that they can write not just for their own intimates but for wider audiences. Teachers will want to engage in respectful inquiry with students about significant differences between patterns in their use of their first language and more conventionally written English. Even as they move toward more widely used English, writers find that it is not necessary or desirable to eliminate the ways their family and people in their neighborhood use words to express themselves. The teaching of excellence in writing means adding language to what already exists, not subtracting. Further, expert writing teachers deliberately teach students to incorporate their heritage and home languages intentionally and strategically in the texts they write. The goal is to make more relationships available, not fewer.

In order to provide high-quality writing opportunities for all students, teachers need to understand:

- How to find out about students' language use in the home and their neighborhoods, the changes in language context they may have encountered in their lives, and the kinds of language they most value;

- The ways wider social situations in which students speak, write, read, and relate to other people affect what feels to them natural or unnatural, easy or hard;

- How mixing languages within a text can promote students' acquisition of academic language, deeper competence in a repertoire of codes, ability to communicate complex thoughts, and ways of communicating with various audiences;

Professional Knowledge for the Teaching of Writing

- How teachers who do not speak or understand a student's home language can embrace and support the use of home languages in the classroom;
- How to discuss respectfully with students expectations for flexibility in the employment of different kinds of language for different social contexts in order to gain access to some powerful social worlds;
- How to help students negotiate maintenance of their most familiar and cherished language practices while developing strength in academic classroom English;
- Control and awareness of their own varied and strategic ways of using language and the social contexts that expect them;
- An understanding of the relationships among group affiliation, identity, and language;
- Knowledge of the usual patterns of common dialects in English, such as African American English, Spanish, and varieties of English related to Spanish, common patterns in American rural and urban populations, predictable patterns in the English varieties of groups common in their teaching contexts;
- The online spaces through which students communicate, and how their uses of digitalk differs from conventional written English.

Related:
CCCC Statement on Second Language Writing and Writers [2]
Resolution on the Student's Right to Incorporate Heritage and Home Languages in Writing [3]

Composing occurs in different modalities and technologies

Composing has always required technology, whether it's the technology we associate with print—including pens, pencils, and paper—or the technology we associate with the digital—including word processors, digital imaging software, and the Internet. Like all texts, print texts are multimodal: print, whether hand-created or machine-produced, relies for meaning on multiple modalities, including language, layout, and the visual characteristics of the script. Moreover, print has often included visuals—including maps, line drawings, illustrations, and graphs—to create a fuller representation of meaning, to tap the familiarity of a visual to help readers make meaning in a new genre, to add aesthetic value, and to appeal to a wider audience. Film, television, and video involve such combinations of modalities, as do presentation software and websites. As technologies for composing have expanded, "composing" has increasingly referred to a suite of activities in varied modalities. Composers today work with many modalities, including language, layout, still images, other visuals, video, and sound. Computers, both the stationary and mobile varieties, provide a work environment where composers can employ and combine these modalities. Moreover, the Internet not only makes a range of new and diverse materials available to writers, but also brings writers and readers closer together and makes possible new kinds of collaborations. Thus, when students have access to a computer with full Internet access, composing opportunities expand.

Additionally, increased access to various modalities and technologies has created opportunities for students with a wide range of abilities, backgrounds, and languages to compose with more independence and agency. As more digital tools become available, and more forms of expression are not only accepted but expected, more students are able to employ these tools independently.

What does this mean for teaching?

Writing instruction should support students as they compose with a variety of modalities and technologies. Because students will, in the wider world, be using word processing for drafting, revision, and editing, incorporating visual components in some compositions, and including links where appropriate, definitions of composing should include these practices; definitions that exclude them are out-of-date and inappropriate.

Because many teachers and students do not have access to the most up-to-date technologies, such as portable devices with cameras, teaching students to compose multimodally may best be accomplished by foregrounding multimodal dimensions of composing in low-tech environments. An assignment for students to create picture books, for example, can allow them to consider how languages and images complement each other and assist the reader. Similar kinds of visual/verbal thinking can be supported across the school curriculum through other illustrated text forms, including journals, design notebooks, and posters. Attention to modalities in assignments and genres like these demonstrates the extent to which "new" literacies are rooted in older ones.

In order to provide high-quality writing opportunities for all students, teachers need to understand:

- A range of new genres that have emerged on the Internet;
- Open-source platforms that students can use for composing and electronic portfolios;
- Design and layout principles for print and digital publication;
- Conventions for digital communication, including email, chat, text messages, social networking, and online discussion forums;
- Ways to navigate both the World Wide Web and Web-based databases;
- Ways to access, evaluate, use, and cite information found on the Internet;
- Theory about and history of modalities, technologies, and the affordances they offer for meaning making;
- Operation of hardware and software that composers use, including resources for solving software and hardware problems;
- Tools that help students compose as independently as possible, in the modalities that best fit their needs and purposes;
- Internet resources for remaining up-to-date on technologies.

Related:
Resolution on Composing with Nonprint Media [4]
Position Statement on Multimodal Literacies [5]
CCCC Position Statement on Teaching, Learning, and Assessing Writing in Digital Environments [6]

Professional Knowledge for the Teaching of Writing

21st-Century Literacies: A Policy Research Brief [7]

Conventions of finished and edited texts are an important dimension of the relationship between writers and readers.

Readers expect writing to conform to their expectations. For public texts written for a general audience, contemporary readers expect words to be spelled in a standardized way, for punctuation to be used in predictable ways, for usage and syntax to match that used in texts they already acknowledged as successful. They expect the style in a piece of writing to be appropriate to its genre and social situation. With that in mind, writers try to use these surface elements strategically, in order to present the identity, create the relationships, and express the ideas that suit their purpose.

What does this mean for teaching?

Every teacher has to resolve a tension between writing as generating and shaping ideas and writing as a final product, demonstrating expected surface conventions. On the one hand, it is important for writing to be as correct as possible and for students to be able to produce correct texts so that readers can read and make meaning from them. On the other hand, achieving correctness is only one set of things writers must be able to do; a correct document empty of ideas or unsuited to its audience or purpose is not a good piece of writing. There is no formula for resolving this tension. Though it may be desirable both fluently to produce writing and to adhere to conventions, growth in fluency and control of conventions may not occur at the same time. If a student's mental energies are focused on new intellectual challenges, he or she may attend less fully to details of grammar and punctuation.

Such uneven development should be tolerated and, in fact, encouraged. Too much emphasis on correctness can actually inhibit a writer's development. By the same token, without mastering conventions for written discourse, writers may find their efforts regarded less highly by readers they had wanted to influence. Each teacher must be knowledgeable enough about the entire landscape of writing instruction to guide particular students toward a goal, including increasing fluency in new contexts, mastering conventions, and perhaps most important, developing rhetorical sophistication and appropriateness—all of which work together. NCTE's stated policy over many years has been that conventions of writing are best taught in the context of writing.

Most writing teachers teach students how to edit their writing that will be shared with audiences. This is often considered a late stage in the process of composing, because editing is only essential for the words, visuals, and other materials that are left after all the cutting, replacing, rewriting, and adding that go on during revision. Writers keep an image in their minds of conventional grammar, spelling, and punctuation in order to compare what is already on the page to what their audience expects. They also need to be aware of stylistic options and larger language choices that will best articulate their ideas and produce the most desirable impression on their readers. Language choices may be a matter of the identity a writer seeks to project, and those identities may not be productively standardized. In digital environments, there may be an expected way of using language due to the nature of the

Professional Knowledge for the Teaching of Writing

platform, such as in texting or blogging, where the conventional usage might differ from language in other contexts.

An area of consideration with respect to conventions in writing is the development of language proficiency for students learning English as an additional language. Experienced teachers understand that these multilingual students will enter the classroom at different stages and vary in the pace with which they acquire their new language. Knowledge of students' cultural and linguistic background and the way that background intersects or differs from English language conventions helps ensure that students are receiving instruction appropriate for their current stage of language learning. Writers who are learning English as an additional language will have multiple possible patterns in mind for phonology, morphology, syntax, and often genre and pragmatics as well. That is, they know more, and are sorting through that knowledge. Some may require support in analyzing the expectations of a wider English-dominant audience in contrast to the patterns of their earlier language(s). For many, patterns from the first language will persist and should be treated with the respect and generosity that should be afforded to spoken accented English.

In order to provide high-quality writing opportunities for all students, teachers need to understand:

- Developmental factors in writing, including the tension between fluency with new operations or content and the practices that produce accepted spelling, punctuation, syntactic, and usage conventions;

- Diverse influences and constraints on writers' decision making as they determine the conventions that apply to this situation and this piece of writing;

- A variety of applications and options for most conventions;

- Appropriate conventions for writing for a particular public audience;

- Linguistic terminology that is helpful for teaching particular kinds of usage without employing excessive linguistic terminology;

- Linguistic terminology helpful for communicating professionally with other educators;

- The relationship among rhetorical considerations and decisions about conventions, for example, the conditions under which a dash, a comma, a semicolon, or a full stop might be more effective;

- Conventions beyond the sentence, such as effective uses of bulleted lists, mixed genres and voices, diagrams and charts, design of pages, and composition of video shots;

- The conditions under which people learn to participate in new social situations, both personal and professional, with language;

- How to understand technologies such as grammar and spelling checkers to decide which changes are applicable in a given editing situation.

Related:

Students' Right to Their Own Language [8]

CCCC Statement on Second Language Writers and Writing [2]

Professional Knowledge for the Teaching of Writing

Everyone has the capacity to write; writing can be taught; and teachers can help students become better writers.

Developing writers require support. This support can best come through carefully designed writing instruction oriented toward acquiring new strategies and skills. Certainly, writers can benefit from teachers who simply support and give them time to write. However, high-quality instruction matters. Teachers of writing should be well versed in composition theory and research, and they should know methods for turning that theory into practice. They should be capable of teaching writing in both print and digital environments.

Students are different from one another, and they bring to the experience of writing a wide range of resources and strengths. At the same time, any writer can be positioned as weak, struggling, or incompetent. All writers need to learn multiple strategies and modalities to compensate for moments when they feel stuck or defeated, to get on with the business of composing.

As is the case with many activities, becoming a better writer requires that students write. This means actual writing for real audiences, not merely listening to lectures about writing, doing grammar drills, or discussing readings. The more people write, the more familiar it becomes and the more they are motivated to do it. Writers learn from each session with their hands on a keyboard or fingers on a pencil as they draft, rethink, revise, and draft again. Improvement is built into the experience of writing when writers revise, strategizing ways to make their writing better.

What does this mean for teaching?

Writing instruction must include ample in-class and out-of-class opportunities for writing, including writing in digital spaces, and should involve writing for a variety of purposes and audiences, including audiences beyond the classroom. Teachers need to support students in the development of writing lives, habits, and preferences for life outside school. We already know that many students do extensive amounts of self-sponsored writing: emailing, keeping journals or doing creative projects, instant messaging, making websites, blogging, creating fan fiction. Though critically important for college and career, the teaching of writing should also be geared toward making sense in a life outside of school, so that writing has ample room to grow in individuals' lives. It is useful for teachers to consider what elements of their curriculum they could imagine students self-sponsoring outside school. Ultimately, those are the activities that will produce more writing.

In order to provide high-quality writing opportunities for all students, teachers need to understand:

- How to interpret curriculum documents, including standards, skills, strategies, concepts, and content that can be taught while students are actually writing, rather than one dimension of composing at a time to all students at once;
- How to create writing lives for the world beyond school;
- How to construct social structures that support independent work;
- How to confer with individual writers;

Professional Knowledge for the Teaching of Writing

- How to assess students' work while they are in the process of writing—formatively—in order to offer timely assistance during the composing process;
- How to plan what students need to know in response to ongoing research;
- How to create a sense of community and personal safety in the classroom, so that students are willing to write and collaborate freely and at length;
- How to effectively employ a variety of technologies such as brainstorming tools, collaborative word processors, and bibliography managers for students to engage in writing fully;
- How to ensure that every student has the tools and supports necessary to be as independent as possible;
- How to encourage and include students writing in their home languages.

Related:
NCTE Beliefs about Students' Right to Write [9]
Resolution on Students' Right of Expression [10]
What We Know about Writing, Grades K–2 [11]
How to Help Your Child Become a Better Writer (English) [12]
How to Help Your Child Become a Better Writer (Español) [13]

Writing is a process.

Often, when people think of writing, they think of texts—finished pieces of writing that stand alone. Understanding what writers do, however, involves both thinking about what texts look like when they are finished as well as thinking about what strategies writers might employ to produce those texts, especially when using a variety of technologies. Knowledge about writing is only complete when writers understand the ensemble of actions in which they engage as they produce texts. Such understanding has two aspects, at least. First is the development, through extended practice over years, of a repertory of routines, skills, strategies, and practices, for generating, revising, and editing different kinds of texts. Second is the development of reflective abilities and meta-awareness about writing. The procedural knowledge developed through reflective practice helps writers most when they encounter difficulty, or when they are in the middle of creating a piece of writing. How does someone get started? What do they do when they get stuck? How do they plan the overall process, each section of their work, and even the rest of the sentence they are writing right now? Research, theory, and practice in the teaching of writing have produced a rich understanding of what writers do, those who are proficient and professional as well as those who struggle.

Two further points are vital. First, to say that writing is a process is decidedly not to say that it should—or can—be turned into a formulaic set of steps or reduced to a set of traits. Experienced writers shift between different operations according to their audience, the purpose of the writing task, the genre, and circumstances, such as deadlines and considerations of length, style, and format.

Second, writers do not accumulate process skills and strategies once and for all. They develop and refine writing skills throughout their writing lives, as they take up new tasks

Professional Knowledge for the Teaching of Writing

in new genres for new audiences. They grow continually, across personal and professional contexts, using numerous writing spaces and technologies.

What does this mean for teaching?

Whenever possible, teachers should attend to the process that students might follow to produce texts—and not only specify criteria for evaluating finished products, in form or content. Students should become comfortable with prewriting techniques, multiple strategies for developing and organizing a message, a variety of strategies for revising and editing, and methods for preparing products for public audiences and for deadlines. In explaining assignments, teachers should provide guidance and options for ways of accomplishing the objectives. Using formative assessment to understand the processes students follow—the decisions they make, the attempts along the way—can be at least as important as evaluating the final product with a holistic score or grade. Moreover, they should understand how various digital writing tools—mind mapping, word processing, bibliography managers—can be employed in academically useful ways. At least some of the time, the teacher should guide the students through the process, assisting them as they go. Writing instruction must provide opportunities for students to identify the processes that work best for themselves as they move from one initial idea to final draft, from one writing situation to another.

Writing instruction must also take into account that a good deal of workplace writing and other writing takes place in collaborative situations. Writers must learn to work effectively with one another to create writing, provide feedback, and complete a final draft, often with the use of collaborative technologies.

In order to provide high-quality writing opportunities for all students, teachers need to understand:

- The relationship between features of finished writing and the actions writers perform to create that writing;
- What writers of different genres, including political arguments, stories, poems, blog posts, technical reports, and more, say about their craft;
- The process of writing from the inside, that is, what the teachers themselves as writers experience in a host of different writing situations;
- Multiple strategies for approaching a wide range of typical problems writers face during composing, including strategies for invention, audience, and task analysis, incorporation of images and other visuals, revision, and editing;
- Multiple, flexible models of the writing process, the varied ways individuals approach similar tasks, and the ways that writing situations and genres inform processes;
- How to design time and possibly staged intervals of work for students to do their best work on a given assignment;
- A range of digital writing tools that writers might find useful in their processes, including word processors, databases, outliners, mind mapping software, design software, shared-document websites, and other hardware, software, and Web-based technologies.

Professional Knowledge for the Teaching of Writing

Related:
Framework for Success in Postsecondary Writing [14]
CCCC Principles for the Postsecondary Teaching of Writing [15]

Writing is a tool for thinking.

When writers actually write, they think of things that they did not have in mind before they began writing. The act of writing generates ideas; writing can be an act of discovery. This is different from the way we often think of writers—as the solitary author who works diligently to get ideas fixed in his or her head before writing them down. The notion that writing is a medium for thought is important in several ways and suggests a number of important uses for writing: to solve problems, to identify issues, to construct questions, to reconsider something one had already figured out, to try out a half-baked idea. This insight that writing is a tool for thinking helps us to understand the process of drafting and revision as one of exploration, and is nothing like the idea of writing as transcribing from prerecorded tape. Nor is the writing process simply fixing the mistakes in an early draft; rather, it involves finding more and more wrinkles and implications in what one is talking about.

What does this mean for teaching?

In any writing classroom, some of the writing is for the writer and some for other audiences as well. Regardless of the age, ability, or experience of the writer, the use of writing to generate thought is still valuable; therefore, forms of writing such as personal narrative, journals, written reflections, observations, and writing-to-learn strategies should be included in the curriculum.

In order to provide high-quality writing opportunities for all students, teachers need to understand:

- How to employ varied tools for thinking through writing, such as journals, writers' notebooks, blogs, sketchbooks, digital portfolios, listservs or online discussion groups, dialogue journals, double-entry or dialectical journals, and others;

- The kinds of new thinking—such as questioning, discovery, and invention—that occur when writers revise;

- The varieties of thinking people do when they compose, and what those types of thinking look like when they appear in writing;

- Strategies for getting started with an idea, or finding an idea when one does not occur immediately;

- Exploring various technologies such as drawing tools and voice-to-text translators for brainstorming and developing one's initial thinking;

- Ways to accommodate differences among students, such as those who find writing physically challenging, by using oral rehearsal of ideas, gesture, diagramming, or other options that would still allow exploration and development of thought.

Professional Knowledge for the Teaching of Writing

Related:
Resolution on Writing Across the Curriculum [16]

Writing has a complex relationship to talk.

From its beginnings in early childhood, through K–2 and college classrooms, and throughout a variety of workplaces and community settings, writing exists in an environment of talk. Speakers often write notes or scripts. Writers often talk in order to rehearse the language and content that will go into what they write, and conversation often provides an impetus or occasion for writing. Writers sometimes confer with teachers and other writers about what to do next, how to improve their drafts, or how to clarify their ideas and purposes. Their usual ways of speaking either may or may not feed into the sentences they write, depending on intricate, continuous, important decisions.

What does this mean for teaching?

In early childhood, teachers expect lots of talk to surround writing, since children are figuring out how to get speech onto paper. Early teaching in composition should also attend to helping children get used to producing language orally, through telling stories, explaining how things work, predicting what will happen, and guessing about why things and people are the way they are. Early writing experiences will often include students explaining orally what is in a text, whether it is printed or drawn.

As they grow, writers still need opportunities to talk about what they are writing about, to rehearse the language of their upcoming texts and run ideas by trusted colleagues before and as they take the risk of committing words to paper. After making a draft, it is often helpful for writers to discuss with peers what they have done, partly in order to get ideas from their peers, partly to see what they, the writers, say when they try to explain their thinking. Writing conferences, wherein student writers talk about their work with a teacher, who can make suggestions or reorient what the writer is doing, are also very helpful uses of talk in the writing process.

In order to provide high-quality writing opportunities for all students, teachers need to understand:

- Ways of setting up and managing student talk in partnerships and groups;
- Ways of establishing a balance between talk and writing in classroom management;
- Ways of organizing the classroom and/or schedule to permit individual teacher-student conferences;
- Strategies for deliberate insertions of opportunities for talk into the writing process: knowing when and how students should talk about their writing;
- Ways of anticipating and solving interpersonal conflicts that arise when students discuss writing;
- Relationships—both similarities and differences—between oral and literate language;
- The uses of writing in public presentations and the values of students making oral presentations that grow out of and use their writing;

Professional Knowledge for the Teaching of Writing

- How technologies such as voice recording apps on smartphones and audio editing tools can be used as students create podcasts, videos, or other multimedia work in which they share their writing through oral production.

Related:
What We Know about Writing, Grades 3–5 [17]
What We Know about Writing, Grades 6–8 [18]

Writing and reading are related.

Writing and reading are related. People who engage in considerable reading often find writing an easier task, though the primary way a writer improves is through writing. Still, it's self-evident that to write a particular kind of text, it helps if the writer has read that kind of text, if only because the writer then has a mental model of the genre. In order to take on a particular style of language, it also helps to have read that language, to have heard it in one's mind, so that one can hear it again in order to compose it.

Writing can also help people become better readers. In their earliest writing experiences, children listen for the relationships of sounds to letters, which contributes greatly to their phonemic awareness and phonics knowledge. Writers also must learn how texts are structured, because eventually they have to compose in different genres, and that knowledge of structure helps them to predict and make sense of the sections and sequencing of the texts they read. The experience of plotting a short story, organizing a research report, or making line breaks in a poem permits the writer, as a reader, to approach new reading experiences with more informed eyes.

Additionally, reading is a vital source of information and ideas. For writers fully to contribute to a given topic or to be effective in a given situation, they must be familiar with and draw on what previous writers have said. Reading also creates a sense of what one's audience knows or expects on a topic.

What does this mean for teaching?

One way teachers help students become better writers is to make sure they have lots of extended time to read, in school and out. Teachers also make sure students have access to and experience in reading material that presents both professionally published and student writing in various genres. If one is going to write in a genre, it is very helpful to have read in that genre first. Overall, frequent conversations about the connections between what we read and what we write are helpful. These connections will sometimes be about the structure and craft of the writing itself, and sometimes about thematic and content connections.

In order to provide high-quality writing opportunities for all students, teachers need to understand:

- How writers read for the purposes of writing—with an eye toward not just what the text says but also how it is put together;
- The psychological and social processes reading and writing have in common;

Professional Knowledge for the Teaching of Writing

- The ways writers imagine their intended readers, anticipating their responses and needs;
- That text structures are fluid enough to accommodate frequent exceptions, innovations, and disruptions;
- How writers can identify mentor or exemplar texts, both print and digital, that they may want to emulate in their own writing.

Related:
On Reading, Learning to Read, and Effective Reading Instruction [19]
Reading and Writing Across the Curriculum: A Policy Research Brief [20]
Framework for Success in Postsecondary Writing [21]

Assessment of writing involves complex, informed, human judgment.

Assessment of writing occurs for different purposes. The most fundamental and important assessment of writing is that of the writer, whose efficacy and growth demands that she or he determine and intend what to work on next, throughout the process of producing a single text and across experiences as she or he grows through a writing life. Sometimes, a teacher assesses in order to decide what the student has achieved and what he or she still needs to learn. Sometimes, an agency or institution beyond the classroom assesses a student's level of achievement in order to say whether he or she can go on to some new educational level that requires the writer to be able to do certain things. At other times, school authorities require a writing test as a mechanism for requiring teachers to teach writing, or a certain kind or genre of writing. Still other times, as in a history or literature exam, the assessment of writing itself is not the point, but the quality of the writing is evaluated almost in passing.

In any of these assessments of writing, complex judgments are required. Human beings need to make these judgments, not software programmed to score essays, because only human beings can be sensitive enough to purposes, audience, quality and relevance of evidence, truth in content, and the like. Furthermore, such judgments should be made by professionals who are educated and informed about writing, writing development, the various ways writing can be assessed, and the ways such assessments can support writers.

Instructors of composition should know about various methods of assessment of student writing. Instructors must recognize the difference between formative and summative evaluation and be prepared to evaluate students' writing from both perspectives. By formative evaluation here, we mean provisional, ongoing, in-process judgments about what students know and what to teach next—assessments that may be complex descriptions and not reduced to a grade or score and that are intended to support students' writerly development. By summative evaluation, we mean final judgments about the quality of student work (typically reflected in a grade).

In order to provide high-quality writing opportunities for all students, teachers need to understand:

- How to find out what student writers can do, informally, on an ongoing basis;
- How to use that assessment in order to decide what and how to teach next;
- How to assess occasionally, less frequently, in order to form and report judgments about the quality of student writing and learning;

Professional Knowledge for the Teaching of Writing

- How to assess ability and knowledge across multiple different writing engagements;
- What the features of good writing are, appropriate to the context and purposes of the teaching and learning;
- What the elements of a constructive process of writing are, appropriate to the context and purposes of the teaching and learning;
- What growth in writing looks like, the developmental aspects of writing ability;
- Ways of assessing student metacognitive process as they connect writing to reading;
- How to recognize in student writing (in both their texts and their actions) the nascent potential for excellence at the features and processes desired;
- How to deliver useful feedback, appropriate for the writer and the situation;
- How to analyze writing situations for their most essential elements, so that assessment is not of everything about writing all at once, but rather is targeted to outcomes;
- How to analyze and interpret both qualitative and quantitative writing assessments and make decisions about their usefulness;
- How to evaluate electronic texts;
- How to use portfolios to assist writers in their development and how to assess portfolios;
- How self-assessment and reflection contribute to a writer's development and ability to move among genres, media, and rhetorical situations;
- How to employ a variety of technologies—including screencasting and annotation, embedded text and voice comments, and learning management systems—to provide timely, useful, and goal-oriented feedback to students.

Related:
Writing Assessment: A Position Statement of CCCC [22]
NCTE Position Statement on Machine Scoring [23]
NCTE Resolution on Grading Student Writing [24]

This position statement may be printed, copied, and disseminated without permission from NCTE.

Article printed from NCTE: **https://ncte.org**
URL to article: **https://ncte.org/statement/teaching-writing/**
URLs in this post:
[1] *Writing Now: A Policy Research Brief Produced by the National Council of Teachers of English*: **https://secure.ncte.org/library/NCTEFiles/Resources/Journals/CC/0181-sept2008/CC0181Policy.pdf**
[2] *CCCC Statement on Second Language Writing and Writers*: **https://cccc.ncte.org/cccc/resources/positions/secondlangwriting**
[3] *Resolution on the Student's Right to Incorporate Heritage and Home Languages in Writing*: **https://ncte.org/statement/homelanguages/**
[4] *Resolution on Composing with Nonprint Media*: **https://ncte.org/statement/composewithnonprint/**

Professional Knowledge for the Teaching of Writing

[5] *Position Statement on Multimodal Literacies*: **https://ncte.org/statement/multimodal literacies/**

[6] *CCCC Position Statement on Teaching, Learning, and Assessing Writing in Digital Environments*: **https://cccc.ncte.org/cccc/resources/positions/digitalenvironments**

[7] *21st-Century Literacies: A Policy Research Brief*: **https://secure.ncte.org/library/ NCTEFiles/Resources/Positions/Chron1107ResearchBrief.pdf**

[8] *Students' Right to Their Own Language*: **https://cccc.ncte.org/cccc/resources/positions/ srtolsummary**

[9] *NCTE Beliefs about Students' Right to Write*: **https://ncte.org/statement/students-right-to-write/**

[10] *Resolution on Students' Right of Expression*: **https://ncte.org/statement/rightof expression/**

[11] What We Know about Writing, Grades K–2: **http://www.ncte.org/writing/ aboutearlygrades**

[12]* *How to Help Your Child Become a Better Writer (English)*: **https://ncte.org/statement/ howtohelpenglish/**

[13] *How to Help Your Child Become a Better Writer (Español)*: **https://ncte.org/statement/ howtohelpspanish/**

[14] *Framework for Success in Postsecondary Writing*: **http://wpacouncil.org/framework**

[15] *CCCC Principles for the Postsecondary Teaching of Writing*: **https://cccc.ncte.org/cccc/ resources/positions/postsecondarywriting#principle5**

[16] *Resolution on Writing Across the Curriculum*: **https://www2.ncte.org/statement/ writingacrossthecurr/**

[17] *What We Know about Writing, Grades 3–5*: **http://www.ncte.org/writing/aboutelem**

[18] *What We Know about Writing, Grades 6–8*: **http://www.ncte.org/writing/aboutmiddle**

[19] *On Reading, Learning to Read, and Effective Reading Instruction*: **https://ncte.org/ statement/onreading/**

[20] *Reading and Writing Across the Curriculum: A Policy Research Brief*: **https://secure.ncte .org/library/NCTEFiles/Resources/Journals/CC/0203-mar2011/CC0203Policy.pdf**

[21] *Framework for Success in Postsecondary Writing*: **http://wpacouncil.org/files/frame work-for-success-postsecondary-writing.pdf**

[22] *Writing Assessment: A Position Statement of CCCC*: **https://cccc.ncte.org/cccc/resources/ positions/writingassessment**

[23] *NCTE Position Statement on Machine Scoring*: **https://ncte.org/statement/machine_ scoring/**

[24] *NCTE Resolution on Grading Student Writing*: **https://ncte.org/statement/grading studentwrit/**

*This resource was revised in 2018 and is now titled *Parents as Partners in Promoting Writing among Children and Youth*. The original URL is still good.

Introduction: What's Your Why? Middle Level Kids Writing Themselves into the World

Shelbie Witte

It's important to begin any discussion or conversation about writing and the teaching of writing with the acknowledgment of our "why." Why do we write? The truth is that writing is and has been at the very center of who we are as people. Throughout literate human history, we've used writing to negotiate what it means to be a person, a family, a community, and even a country. We've used symbols and alphabet and moving image to depict narratives, construct arguments, explain processes, and imagine worlds of possibilities that have propelled us forward. We've used writing to find the peace in world conflicts, to track and experiment the cures for disease and the path of discovery, and to document the present for future generations. What a privilege it is to be a teacher of something so vital to what it means to be human.

Who Are We?

I have the great privilege of being an educator. Before my current position as a teacher educator, I was thrilled to spend many years as a middle school ELA National Board Certified teacher in Oklahoma and Kansas, where I was deeply involved in the local National Writing Project (NWP) sites. We might want to pause here to do a close reading of the previous sentence, as it is loaded with important lenses that I bring with me to this project. While I am not currently teaching in a middle level classroom, you will find my heart is there. Most of my professional work is with middle level teachers and with middle schools, and I am proud of my current editorship, along with Sara Kajder, of one of the National Council of Teachers of English's premier journals, *Voices from the Middle*. My time spent writing alongside my middle level students is certainly one of the highlights of my teaching career and even of my life.

I am joined in this book by seven middle level educators who each brings with them their own journeys and their own life experiences to this project. I brought with me to this project some of the very best middle level educators I know, including Sarah Bonner, Illinois, and Margaret A. Robbins, Georgia, who are "on fire" for the endless possibilities of creative, project-based learning in the classroom, and Frances Lin, California, a leader in the Middle Level Section of the National Council of Teachers of English (NCTE) and a writer and mentor for her students. I first came to know Tracei Willis, Mississippi, through our mutual friend Wendy Warren and then face to face at the NWP Annual Meeting in St. Louis, Missouri, in 2017, where Tracei shared during the morning plenary her life-changing experience with The Olga Lengyel Institute for Holocaust Studies and Human Rights (TOLI). I had the pleasure of meeting two tremendous New Jersey educators, Lauren Zucker and Joseph S. Pizzo, at the NCTE Annual Convention a few years ago and have enjoyed following them both through social media spaces as they share their smart thinking with all of us. And finally, I was thrilled that Matthew Homrich-Knieling, Michigan, a Linda Rief *Voices from the Middle* Award winner, accepted the invitation to share his approach to critically sustaining pedagogy through public narratives. These teachers, from diverse settings and with diverse backgrounds, center writing in their classrooms and think carefully and critically about what it means to be a teacher of writing.

It's also important for us to acknowledge here a shared understanding of middle level students. For the purposes of this project, we share many common experiences as middle school teachers and are unapologetic in our embrace of middle level kids as unexpected and unique as human beings can be; middle level kids are multidimensional, multiemotional, multitalented creatures of curiosity and confusion fueled by gusto, hormones, and a little bit of magic. We acknowledge that "our teaching and learning lives are marked daily by the unrelenting energy, sharp quirkiness, and knotty complexities that middle grades youth bring to our every interaction" (Kajder & Witte, 2016, p. 7). Nancie Atwell describes middle level learners as being "on the verge of everything good: purposeful self-expression, serious curiosity about the world and how it works, a sense of humor and a sense of style, tolerance, compassion even, and their own identities" (2016, p. 9). Throughout the chapters in this collection, you will see multiple examples of middle level learners on the verge of everything good, and their teachers working tirelessly to help them get there.

Professional Knowledge for the Teaching of Writing

Ten years ago, NCTE established October 20 as the National Day on Writing, and since that day, thousands of people, adults and children alike, have shared their "whys" to a broader audience through the #WhyIWrite initiative (https://whyiwrite.us/). Not only has #WhyIWrite provided a way to capture a snapshot of what writing looks like in the twenty-first century, but it has also drawn attention to the broader understanding of what it means *be* a writer. In the past decade, changes in culture and technological advancements and access have made visible the importance of writing and writing well. And for us as teachers of writing, this movement and writing visibility offers a "why" *for* our work with our students: we write and teach writing because being a writer is part of being in the world. And this impetus served as the driving force behind the creation of NCTE's *Professional Knowledge for the Teaching of Writing* position statement.

NCTE's *Professional Knowledge for the Teaching of Writing* statement (PKTW), written and adopted in 2016, guides teachers in understanding how the larger picture of the art and craft of writing is directly impacted by the writing pedagogy we use with students in our classrooms. Since NCTE wrote the original *Beliefs about the Teaching of Writing* statement in 2004, the ways in which we engage with writing opportunities have increased dramatically in that "the ways writing and the spoken voice are mutually supportive in writing processes have become increasingly facilitated by technological capabilities" (PKTW, p. ix; the page references to this document map to the version reprinted in the front matter of this book). Indeed, NCTE reminds us of the dramatic shifting of our communicative worlds and the sometimes contradictory advice we as teachers are given about how to navigate it alongside our students.

The PKTW provides ten professional principles that guide the teaching of writing and that frame our work within this book. While each principle serves an important purpose in the process of becoming a writer, the principles also work together in tandem for a more holistic view to help us understand the pedagogical approaches to teaching writing.

We know from our adult life experiences that **writing grows out of many purposes** (Gardner, 2014; Haddix, 2018; Johnson, 2018; Schleppegrell, 2007). Perhaps most indicative of our current times, middle level learners are learning not only the art and craft of writing, but also a great deal about the multitude of ways that writing is important to being a person. From everyday informal writing tasks such as lists and recipes to more formalized writing events for academic purposes, "it is important that students have experiences within school that teach them how writing differs with purpose, audience, and other elements of the situation" (PKTW, p. x). A type of situational literacy, understanding purpose and audience is a skill that builds over time and requires in addition the ability to recognize a mismatch in message and target audience. This becomes complicated as we consider that **writing is embedded in complex social relationships and their appropriate languages** (Garcia & O'Donnell-Allen, 2016; Graham et al., 2016; Janks, 2009; Krishnan et al., 2018; Mirra, 2018). The language we use matters, and the social contexts in which the language is read and understood also matter. We cannot consider our writing in isolation, as the relationship between writer and audience is as complex as the languages we use. Additionally, the social aspect of writing in a community of writers brings with it the added dimension of the writer, the reader, and all relevant others living in "a structured social order, where some people's words count more than others, where being heard is more difficult for some people than others, where some people's words come true and others' do not" (PKTW, p. xi). As we negotiate writing workshops and peer responding, these social spaces are complicated by these dynamics and add to the layers of emotion embedded in what it means to share our writing publicly with others and to receive both praise and critique in the process.

Adding dimensions of complexity to the ways in which we write is the fact that **composing occurs in different modalities and technologies** (Coiro et al., 2014; Hicks & Turner, 2013; Howell et al., 2017). The twenty-first century is robust in its opportunities for students to engage in literacy activities and to become more active citizens than has ever before been possible in our history. The ways in which we compose have expanded dramatically, with new practices and vocabularies at our fingertips. Transmodal messages shared through written word, digital image, or short video and audio are instantaneously available to the world through social media channels, while research reports and entire novels are being written with iPhones and thumbs (according to Weinberger [2016], author Jeff Zentner wrote *The Serpent King* on his iPhone). The implications for writing pedagogy are simultaneously frightening and full of potential for guiding students to a deeper understanding of the power and influence these technologies afford them, as well as the impact their words can have on individuals as well as on society. Our "increased access to various modalities and technologies has created opportunities for students with a wide range of abilities, backgrounds, and languages to compose with more independence and agency" (PKTW, pp. xii–xiii).

The instantaneous nature of writing and publishing in digital environments brings forward more discussion about the tensions related to **conventions of finished and edited texts as an important dimension of the relationship between writers and readers** (MacArthur, 2018; Sommers, 1980; Witte, 2013). Teachers of writing work earnestly to strike a delicate balance between promoting student writers' unfettered flow of ideas and teaching the standardization of language conventions that a writer must internalize in order to be better understood. This balance is difficult to achieve. In fact, "each teacher must be knowledgeable enough about the entire landscape of writing instruction to guide particular students toward a goal, including increasing fluency in new contexts, mastering conventions, and perhaps most important, developing rhetorical sophistication and appropriateness—all of which work together" (PTKW p. xiv). Facilitating opportunities for new thinking while guiding revision and editing work is both an art and a craft.

Ultimately, at the heart of our work as teachers of writing, we must embrace the philosophy that **everyone has the capacity to write; writing can be taught; and teachers can help students become better writers** (Atwell, 1987; Calkins, 1986; Certo et al., 2012). We know from decades of experience that the best teachers of writing are writers themselves, which is the founding philosophy of the National Writing Project (NWP). We also know that effective writing teachers know and understand the theories of composition and know how to translate those theories into practice. In addition, we need to recognize that all writers, even gifted ones, can be characterized as struggling in many contexts and new writing situations. Ultimately, "writers need to learn multiple strategies and modalities to compensate for moments when they feel stuck or defeated, to get on with the business of composing" (PKTW, p. xvi). We need to make visible our own writing strategies, modeling and mentoring our students alongside our own work, and highlighting the lifelong journey of being a writer. We also need to be unequivocally insistent about taking the necessary time in our classrooms to develop our students' capacity to be writers. We value what we spend time doing; writing matters. And because **writing is a process** (Bazerman, 2013; Emig, 1971; Flower & Hayes, 1981; MacArthur et al., 2013), having the time necessary to do the work of writing development is critical. While the concept of a linear process of writing flourished in publications and classrooms in the 1980s, we have since learned to embrace an understanding of the process of writing as more complex and robust, as an individualized approach needing facilitation versus prescriptive dictation of structure. The multiple cognitive processes at play during writing do not happen in a linear fashion. Using skills, strategies, and reflection, people "develop and refine writing skills throughout their writing lives, as they take up new tasks in new genres for new audiences. They grow continually, across personal and professional contexts, using numerous writing spaces and technologies" (PKTW, pp. xvii–xviii). Or more simply put, **writing is a tool for thinking** (Applebee & Langer, 2013; VanDerHeide & Juzwik, 2018). While much of the writing we do in classrooms is for a larger purpose or audience, we need to recognize the importance of the informal writing necessary to understand, to clarify, and to inquire. Putting thoughts on paper provides students the opportunity to visualize their thinking and to evaluate the best next steps to move their thinking forward. It's vital, then, to emphasize and model for students that "the use of writing to generate thought is still valuable; therefore, forms of writing such as personal narrative, journals, written reflections, observations, and writing-to-learn strategies should be included in the curriculum" (PKTW, p. xix).

It's important to also recognize that writing does not happen in a vacuum, for **writing has a complex relationship to talk** (Dutro & Cartun, 2016; VanderHeide, 2018; Vetter & Meacham, 2018) and **writing and reading are related** (Graves, 1991; NWP with DeVoss et al., 2010). Many successful writers talk through their writing ideas with trusted colleagues, and the same is true for students. When students are provided opportunities to discuss, detail, and even defend their writing to groups of their peers, they grow in their understanding of their work. For students, talking about writing is "partly in order to get ideas from their peers, partly to see what they, the writers, say when they try to explain their thinking" (PKTW, p. xx). Also important to the dynamic is the relationship between reading and writing. Not only does reading provide examples of mentor texts for a writer, but becoming well-read on the writing topic allows writers to speak from knowledge and "draw on what previous writers have said" (PKTW, p. xxi). A literacy-rich classroom with diverse texts and genres allows students to become more comfortable with wordplay and to engage in writing that stretches their experiences.

And finally, a discussion about writing principles cannot be complete without acknowledging the reality of the need for effective writing assessment, which embraces the philosophy that **the assessment of writing involves complex, informed, human judgment** (Hillocks, 2002; McGrail & Behizadeh, 2017; Christenbury et al., 2011; Yancey, 1999). Writing assessment, and any assessment for that matter, should be for the benefit of the learner, the individual being assessed. And yet, for the most part, writing instruction in our country is designed as an outcome of the state mandates designed to determine teacher and school success. Unfortunately, part of that movement involves assessing writing with computers programmed to recognize particular algorithmic patterns of "success." The realities of state-mandated assessments may not soon go away, so educators must advocate for multifaceted assessments of our students' writing, evaluated by experienced (not Craigslist-hired) writing professionals who understand the complex, rhetorical, and recursive nature of writing (Strauss, 2013).

Through these ten principles, the PKTW statement provides us with the very best thinking in the study of writing and writing instruction. It serves as a springboard to demonstrating how we actively approach the teaching of writing in our own classrooms and frames our demonstrations of that work in the chapters that follow. In these chapters, we situate our classroom practice with purpose and with a lens on writing that moves thinking forward: writing that "does" work; writing that influences and makes their world a better place, either by helping a middle level student write their way to a better understanding of self or by creating writing that makes social moves within a community and impacts a larger world. The teachers featured here are doing the hard work of teaching writing in ways that focus on these goals. When we can help students become better writers, they become better at expressing their thoughts, defending their ideas, speaking truth to power. In doing so, we have the opportunity to use the writing that we do to make a difference. Writing for social change—for better water conditions, for safer schools . . . all have the potential to make an impact.

In each of these chapters, we provide readers with a glimpse of each teacher's classroom and the "whys" that ground their work with their students. We situate each teaching approach within the PKTW statement and provide examples of how each middle level teacher navigates their approach within these best practices. Ultimately, each teacher shares what works for them, what they would do differently, and how they are continuing to learn and grow from their reflection.

Within each section of this book, we share a writing approach from both a micro and a macro perspective to offer opportunities to consider how each can be accomplished, from a classroom-level perspective to a larger community perspective. In Part I, Writing That Enters the World, we examine what it means for middle level kids to put their writing into the world. In Chapter 1, Frances Lin offers us the micro approach, tackling the difficult task of teaching and fostering revision using the beloved NWP exercise of "Where I'm From" to model her own memoir poetry. For many students, writing memoir is a first step in putting their words on paper for the "world" to see. In Chapter 2, Sarah Bonner shares the macro approach and how project-based learning changed her entire teaching approach as her rural students found purpose in self-driven inquiries that impacted their larger communities.

In Part II, Writing That Moves the World, we examine what middle level kids can do when given the opportunity to take ownership of their writing to express their thinking about complex social issues and to solve problems through sophisticated inquiry projects. Tracei Willis, in Chapter 3, shares the micro approach and delights us with poetic expression and real talk about motivating middle level learners to have difficult discussions about the world, starting with themselves. Chapter 4 highlights the macro approach with Margaret A. Robbins and her middle level students as they share how they discover, define, design, and deploy video and board games for elementary students through design-based critical thinking and composition.

In Part III, Writing That Heals the World, we expand our understanding of the power of what writing can do to heal others and initiate change that can address and even solve some of the world's larger issues. Chapter 5 spotlights Lauren Zucker and Joseph S. Pizzo as they share the micro approach of writing sympathetic expressions of comfort to encourage and prepare students for difficult conversations. And in Chapter 6, Matthew Homrich-Knieling describes the power of pedagogy that recognizes Latinx middle level immigrants as co-designers of their own curriculum through public narratives and writing that *does* the work of healing a world gone wrong, a macro approach.

What resonates most with me in this thoughtful and critical convocation of voices is our collective hope that this book, and our work in it, will give all teachers permission to do the hard work of writing for a purpose—to attempt to try some of the suggested approaches or to stretch and try something new, to guide middle level students to do writing that helps them better understand the world and to better find and stake their places within it. We are cognizant of the fact that teachers come to a book with a wide range of skill sets. Some of you may be seeking assistance with what we would term *traditional* writing instruction approaches, while others of you may be interested in more contemporary, multimodal, and twenty-first-century approaches. Regardless of where you are in your learning, we want each of you to see the possibilities and to say, "I can do this."

Learning Tracker

Reflect on the ten principles of the *Professional Knowledge for the Teaching of Writing* statement. Which principles come easily to you in your teaching? Which principles challenge you as a teacher? How much class time do you allocate for each of the principles? How do these principles align with your students' purposes for writing?

References

Applebee, A. N., & Langer, J. A. (2013). *Writing instruction that works: Proven methods for middle and high school classrooms*. New York, NY: Teachers College Press.

Atwell, N. (1987). *In the middle: Writing, reading, and learning with adolescents*. Portsmouth, NH: Heinemann.

Atwell, N. (2016). How to thrive in the middle. *Voices from the Middle, 24*(2), 9–12.

Bazerman, C. (2013). *A rhetoric of literate action: Literate action* (Vol. I). Fort Collins, CO: The WAC Clearinghouse.

Calkins, L. M. (1986, 1994). *The art of teaching writing*. Portsmouth, NH: Heinemann.

Certo, J. L., Apol, L., Wibbens, E., & Hawkins, L. K. (2012). Living the poet's life: Using an aesthetic approach to poetry to enhance preservice teachers' poetry experiences and dispositions. *English Education, 44*(2), 102–46.

Christenbury, L., Bomer, R., & Smagorinsky, P. (Eds.). (2011). *Handbook of adolescent literacy research*. New York, NY: Guilford Press.

Coiro, J., Knobel, M., Lankshear, C., & Leu, D. J. (2014). *Handbook of research on new literacies*. Abingdon, UK: Routledge.

Dutro, E., & Cartun, A. (2016). Cut to the core practices: Toward visceral disruptions of binaries in practice-based teacher education. *Teaching and Teacher Education*, *58*, 119–28.

Emig, J. (1971). *The composing processes of twelfth graders*. Urbana, IL: NCTE.

Flower, L., & Hayes, J. R. (1981). A cognitive process theory of writing. *College Composition and Communication*, *32*(4), 365–87.

Garcia, A., & O'Donnell-Allen, C. (2016). Wobbling with writing: Challenging existing paradigms of secondary writing instruction and finding new possibilities. *Literacy Research: Theory, Method, and Practice*, *65*(1), 348–64.

Gardner, P. (2014). Becoming a teacher of writing: Primary student teachers reviewing their relationship with writing. *English in Education*, *48*(2), 128–48.

Graham, S., Harris, K. R., & Chambers, A. B. (2016). Evidence-based practice and writing instruction: A Review of Reviews. In C. A. MacArthur, S. Graham, & J. Fitzgerald (Ed.s), *Handbook of writing research* (2nd ed., pp. 211–26). New York, NY: Guilford Press.

Graves, D. H. (1991). *Build a literate classroom*. Portsmouth, NH: Heinemann.

Haddix, M. M. (2018). What's radical about youth writing? Seeing and honoring youth writers and their literacies. *Voices from the Middle*, *25*(3), 8–12.

Hicks, T., & Turner, K. H. (2013). No longer a luxury: Digital literacy can't wait. *English Journal*, *102*(6), 58.

Hillocks, G. (2002). *The testing trap: How state writing assessments control learning*. New York, NY: Teachers College Press.

Howell, E., Butler, T., & Reinking, D. (2017). Integrating multimodal arguments into high school writing instruction. *Journal of Literacy Research*, *49*(2), 181–209.

Janks, H. (2009). *Literacy and power*. New York, NY: Routledge.

Johnson, L. P. (2018). Alternative writing worlds: The possibilities of personal writing for adolescent writers. *Journal of Adolescent & Adult Literacy*, *62*(3), 311–18. http://dx.doi.org/10.1002/jaal.762

Kajder, S., & Witte, S. (2016). Learning that matters. *Voices from the Middle*, *24*(2), 6–7.

Krishnan, J., Cusimano, A., Wang, D., & Yim, S. (2018). Writing together: Online synchronous collaboration in middle school. *Journal of Adolescent & Adult Literacy*, *62*(2), 163–73.

MacArthur, C. A. (2018). Evaluation and revision. In S. Graham, C. A. MacArthur, & M. Hebert (Eds.), *Best practices in writing instruction* (3rd Ed., p. 287). New York, NY: Guilford Press.

MacArthur, C. A., Graham, S., & Fitzgerald, J. (Eds.). (2013). *Best practices in writing instruction* (2nd ed.). New York, NY: Guilford Press.

McGrail, E., & Behizadeh, N. (2017). K–12 multimodal assessment and interactive audiences: An exploratory analysis of existing frameworks. *Assessing Writing*, *31*, 24–38.

Mirra, N. (2018). *Educating for empathy: Literacy learning and civic engagement*. New York, NY: Teachers College Press.

National Council of Teachers of English. (2016). *Professional knowledge for the teaching of writing*. Urbana, IL: Author. Retrieved from http://www2.ncte.org/statement/teaching-writing/

National Writing Project with DeVoss, D. N., Eidman-Aadahl, E., & Hicks, T. (2010). *Because digital writing matters: Improving student writing in online and multimedia environments*. San Francisco, CA: Jossey-Bass.

Schleppegrell, M. (2007). At last: The meaning in grammar. *Research in the Teaching of English*, *42*(1), 121–28. Retrieved from http://www.jstor.org/stable/40171750

Sommers, N. (1980). Revision strategies of student writers and experienced adult writers. *College Composition and Communication*, *31*(4), 378–88.

Strauss, V. (2013). *Pearson criticized for finding test essay scorers on Craigslist*. Retrieved from: https://www.washingtonpost.com/news/answer-sheet/wp/2013/01/16/pearson-criticized-for-finding-test-essay-scorers-on-craigslist/

VanDerHeide, J. (2018). Classroom talk as writing instruction for learning to make writing moves in literary arguments. *Reading Research Quarterly*, *53*(3), 323–44. http://dx.doi.org/10.1002/rrq.196

VanDerHeide, J., & Juzwick, M. M. (2018). Argument as conversation: Students responding through writing to significant conversations across time and place. *Journal of Adolescent and Adult Literacy*, *62*(1), 67–77.

Vetter, A., & Meacham, M. (2018). The significance of reflective conversations for adolescent writers. *English Teaching: Practice & Critique*, *17*(3), 228–44.

Weinberger, A. (2016). *Southern charm and modern technology combine in YA hit "The Serpent King."* Retrieved from: https://mashable.com/2016/03/29/jeff-zentner-serpant-king-interview/#5G09aKozuSqF

Witte, S. (2013). Preaching what we practice. *Journal of Curriculum and Instruction*, *6*(2), 33–59.

Yancey, K. B. (1999). Looking back as we look forward: Historicizing writing assessment. *College Composition and Communication*, *50*(3), 483–503.

Part I
Writing
That Enters
the World

In this section, we highlight two different approaches to writing instruction that gives students the opportunity to write themselves into the world. From the micro perspective, Frances shares how writing with her students and modeling revision strategies allows students to grow confident when sharing their writing with their peers and putting their lives and experiences into the larger classroom community. As Frances introduces her students to memoir poetry, she highlights how writers can use and revisit personal experiences to strengthen their writing practices. From a macro perspective, Sarah offers us a glimpse into the world of Genius Hour with her middle level kids, demonstrating how expanding the walls of the classroom allows students to bring their authentic learning into the community. By offering students choice in their learning topics and approaches, Sarah models the important role of teacher-as-facilitator.

Learning Tracker

Some middle level students may be hesitant to share their writing with others, while some crave opportunities to share writing about topics they care deeply about.

As you read Part I, Writing That Enters the World, consider how you build community within your own classroom. How have you built trust among your students? What steps have you taken to make sure all students feel safe in sharing their writing alongside others? Do you use routines to validate each learner's writing? Are there opportunities to flex your curriculum and your target audience beyond your classroom?

Finding Refuge within Memoir Poetry: Using Mentor Texts to Encourage True Revision

Frances Lin
Altamont Elementary School, Mountain House, CA

I reviewed my revision brainstorms as I sat quietly in my classroom. I had been working on this document for days, going through the revision process that I wanted to model for my students before they wrote their own memoir poetry. I hoped this poetry would inspire them, celebrate their individualism and cultural backgrounds, and encourage tolerance and understanding. I had done a version of this poetry activity before, but this was different. This time I sought to motivate them to share a piece of themselves while finding refuge within poetic language, as I have for so many years. I was ready to share a piece of me, and in turn, find the true spirit within each of my students.

Windmills are scattered throughout the central California hills where my K–12 school district resides. When I first started teaching, this was a one-school district. Now there are six K–8 schools and one high school, all built within my years of teaching here. I helped open three of the K–8 schools, and I have taught in four of them. Two more K–8 schools are currently under construction. Over the years, I have watched this district grow as a rural educational institution. Now it is the highest-performing school district in the county. Bay Area folks started to pay attention to this area years ago as waves of families moved here. This is predominantly a commuter community, where parents have the means to provide school materials in abundance; however, their time is scarce. I just had a Section 504 Plan meeting during which the parents turned to the teachers for support because "our son's teachers see him more than we do." This is a familiar sentiment running through the families in this area. Our students have material provisions, but they are lacking in attention from parents who face a four-hour commute each day. Indeed, our roles as teachers are incredibly important in the lives of our students. They rely on us to know, to understand, and to support them every day.

Ensconced within these hills are my seventh- and eighth-grade classes, where I teach single subject English language arts. The most significant part of our day is the writing workshop, where we convene to discuss the progress of our writing pieces, share our work, provide feedback for one another, and write to discover more about ourselves. Poetry is embedded within our structured writing workshop, and I utilize poetry mentor texts throughout the year for reasons similar to Dorfman and Cappelli's contention that poetry "can develop a sense of compassion and empathy that children need to better understand themselves and their world. Beauty and humanity are inextricably woven together into poetic expression" (2012, p. 5).

In the experiences I share in this chapter, my snapshot of lessons using memoir poetry mentor texts, I make the case for teachers to share their writing with their students and to use sample poetry to inspire their students to compose poetry and embrace revision. Mary Kenner Clover states that "the teacher must be a writer, too" (qtd. in Dorfman & Cappelli, 2012, p. 5). She claims that she has "been most successful as a poetry teacher when I've let my students know from the beginning that I am a writer also" (p. 5).

My purpose in introducing memoir poetry is to capture a glimpse into the lives of my students while at the same time teaching them how to use revision when composing a poem. And after the entire lesson sequence explored here, my students demonstrated an interest both in writing poetry and in revising their work. The poetic vision of my students shone through as they shared themselves and their experiences, even as I was inspired to keep moving forward with my dual focus on poetry mentor texts and revision.

Why Poetry Mentor Texts?

Dorfman and Cappelli define "a mentor text as a piece of writing . . . that you can return to many times in the course of a year and for many reasons. By imitating mentor texts, young writers dare to take risks and try out new things and, as a result, stretch their skills and grow" (2012, p. 8). This exposure to mentor texts—in this case, examples of my own writing—was at the core of my composition and revision lessons. While often teachers use mentor texts to provide students with examples of finished pieces in a particular genre, my goal was to go beyond that: to provide multiple drafts of my own memoir poetry to demonstrate the revision process in action and model for students approaches to analyzing poetic language, imagery, and other writing devices that they might opt to use in their own poetry.

Dorfman and Cappelli also state ten reasons to use poetry as mentor texts, three of which I found to be most notable and relevant to my lessons. First, "poetry can help us see differently, understand ourselves and others, and validate our passions and our human experience" (2012, p. 3). During my poetry lessons, I described much of what makes me who I am, from the traditional Asian cuisines and culture to the Korean War to my philosophical aspirations. Learning about me made my students more introspective and deepened their own self-reflections. Second, "poetry is the great equalizer—a genre especially suited to the struggling or unmotivated reader/writer" (p. 3). Indeed, poetry *was* an equalizer in my lessons. One of the students I highlight in this chapter was a struggling student who was able to take risks for the first time in a long while in my classroom. And finally, "poetry enhances thinking skills and promotes personal connections" (p. 3). My students synthesized my composition and revision process to create their own life stories. Critical thinking and personal connections were an integral part of these poetic experiences in my classroom.

Revision, Teaching as a Writer, and Developing Real Writers

Teaching revision is a complicated task, as we strive to help students find meaning and clear direction in their writing. This is where mentoring *the process* of revision can become an important classroom practice. By sharing their experiences as writers, teachers can equip students with the strategies they can then use when confronted by writing challenges. The modeling of revision within the meaningful context of an authentic writing piece is what truly teaches students about revision because the teacher writer is demonstrating how their own thought process helps them revise. Students need to hear what the writer is thinking and how to work through the parts that confound them.

Importantly, teachers do not need to be published authors to share writing experiences. What is vital, however, is sharing authentic pieces that demonstrate that writing seldom comes out as a finished product in the first draft. Most of us have to endure the somewhat messy process of revision.

Here's how it works in my class: Prior to the delivery of instruction, I always do the writing activity that my students will do. Then, in class, I share my thought process as I go through one of my writing pieces, allowing me to show students how I pull myself out of the quagmire that sometimes threatens to bog me down. I describe specific strategies I use to resolve writing issues, and I show them revision ideas that can improve my original draft. I then confer with students about their writing as well in order to discuss revision possibilities. I focus on them individually and on specific writing issues as we work together to solve problems in their writing. The writing workshop houses all of these events in my classroom and has been a boon for students who want to write better.

Professional Knowledge for the Teaching of Writing

The NCTE *Professional Knowledge for the Teaching of Writing* position statement offers a critical perspective on the teaching of revision through mentor texts. Two elements in particular speak to this idea.

"Everyone has the capacity to write; writing can be taught; and teachers can help students become better writers."

Poetry is certainly an equalizer in the classroom, and as such supports this concept that all students have "the capacity to write." Through my four-week unit on revising memoir poetry, I learned how even my struggling students could embrace revision and compose an end project that overcame their usual disinterest. By providing direct instruction in revision and sharing my poetry as a mentor text, I bridged that gap between the impossible and the possible, thus discovering for myself that writing is possible for every student: writing *can* be taught, and teachers *can* help students become better writers. After delivering instruction, teachers must provide their students with time to write. This benefits all writers. Sharing authentic writing pieces used as mentor texts is an effective way for teachers to teach writing, as well as to help students become better writers. How does a teacher, as a writer, approach a writing piece that is not flowing? What are some strategies that can help students see the process behind making decisions during revision?

"Writing is a process."

Writing is definitely a process, and writing is oftentimes a really long bout of hard work. Demonstrating for students how this process unfolds and what the rewards are is critical so that they understand what various parts of the writing process entail. In this four-week unit, students learned about strategies that could potentially help them revise their writing pieces. They reflected on what they needed support with and conferred with me to resolve writing problems that confronted them. Perhaps one of the hardest things to teach in the writing process is revision. By meticulously retracing my revision steps for my own memoir poetry, I was able to instill in my students the type of revision habits I wanted them to learn and to possess. Students realized that revision is about reflection, contemplation, and creativity. We worked together to face the writing issues we identified and brainstormed to resolve them. The student writing samples discussed later in this chapter highlight how this occurred, through dramatic development from initial drafts to the final drafts. I used memoir poetry to engage students and to entice them into playing with poetic language, which I hoped would feel less threatening than a prose writing piece.

Research That Supports the Use of Memoir Poetry and the Instruction of Revision

Bialosky (2013) explored the fusion of memoir and poetry. These genres, when combined, create a structural ladder of thematic components and intimate connections ascending upward, with voice, poetic language, figurative language, and memories intertwined. When constructing the unit described in this chapter, I thought about Bialosky's work because I wanted to introduce revision in a high-interest writing activity. The memoir poem was an appealing and personal way to entice my young writers to share and to discover how they can develop as writers and poets with the support of a teacher-writer.

Revision research supports the explicit instruction of this part of the writing process as well. The seminal work of Nancy Sommers (1980) involved a case study that traced the revision strategies of inexperienced college writers and of experienced adult writers. Sommers found that the inexperienced writers viewed the process of revision as a "rewording activity" (p. 381); they focused on lexical changes and resorted to the "thesaurus philosophy of writing" (p. 381). Inexperienced students, Sommers noted, looked at lexical repetition but ignored conceptual repetition and semantic changes. In contrast, Sommers discovered, experienced writers looked at purpose, restructuring, and the rewriting of parts that needed clarity. Experienced writers did not follow a linear revision process, but rather pursued a "constant process" developing "like a seed" (p. 378). My goal, aligned with Sommers's research, was to demonstrate how an experienced writer (me!) approaches revision. I shared my thought process, and I worked with students to help them learn these revision strategies as it related to their own writing.

A more recent study by Witte (2013) states that "revision is one of the most difficult things to teach" and that "true revision is also rarely taught" (p. 34). Witte compares the assertions of teacher participants about the teaching of revision before and after a National Writing Project (NWP) institute. According to this study, before the institute, participants expressed confusion about how to even define revision. Many believed there was no difference between revision and editing. Although participants found revision important in their personal writing, "only 30% of participants" spent a "significant amount of time . . . on revision discussions" (p. 41). Revision had a "negative connotation." After engaging in many activities during the institute, participants were much more willing "to spend time on" teaching "revision strategies in the classroom" (p. 44).

Writing Together and Sharing Our Experiences as a Classroom Community

Being open to sharing my writing experiences and providing multiple mentor texts set the tone for our writing workshop during this four-week lesson with a focus on revision. It is important to note, though, that writing immersion is only possible when students have a sense of purpose and personal intention. Students need to feel that they are writing for a purpose beyond grades. I found that their personal stake in their memoir poetry motivated my students to take charge of the revision process I modeled over the four weeks of this unit.

"What is memoir poetry?" I began. Students had various ideas. The words— "autobiography," "writing something personal," "a mix of writing about myself through poetry"—came flying out of my eighth graders. We had studied both genres (memoir and poetry); however, this was the first time we combined them for a writing assignment. We decided as a class that we were going to try to use this hybrid genre to represent who we really are—what expresses us as unique individuals in this world. We wanted to leave an indelible footprint in our classroom and in the world to demonstrate how our lives matter. Grounding my instruction in the much-beloved NWP approach to memoir writing centered on George Ella Lyon's poem "Where I'm From," I proceeded to share the product-based mentor texts— including my own—I had prepared for the lesson. This gave students an idea of what published poets throughout the nation were writing. As students were learning the shape of a memoir poem, I moved on to the mentoring process by sharing a cluster diagram I used when prewriting my first poem (see Figure 1.1).

Figure 1.1. My cluster diagram.

I Am From – Cluster Diagram – Dr. Frances Lin

With this introduction, my students started to create their own cluster diagrams (see Figure 1.2). They also completed their writing workshop tracking sheets each day to trace what they were working on. With the spirit of a writing workshop approach buzzing through the air, students walked up to me to ask questions about their prewriting progress or to get feedback on their ideas. Typically at this point, I'm giving formative feedback. I asked my students what they wanted me

Figure 1.2. A student's cluster diagram.

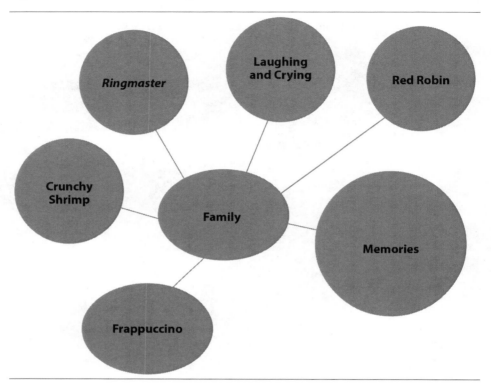

to look for. Some students asked me if they were on the right track, while others had specific questions about their ideas in the cluster diagrams. One student asked me what to do with the different categories, so we reworked the cluster diagram together. I explained that the prewriting process often is about getting ideas on paper and then organizing those ideas. My students enjoyed sharing their ideas and talking about how to approach the poem based on the cluster diagrams.

Revision Brainstorms

At this point, some students were ready to write the first drafts of their memoir poems. I gave students a few days to work on their drafts and then started my revision lesson. I broke up the revision lesson into five parts, mentoring how an experienced writer approaches revision within the specific context of an authentic writing piece. I called the five parts "revision brainstorms," emphasizing that brainstorming revision ideas is just as important as brainstorming in the prewriting stage. Experienced writers, I explained, brainstorm ways to strengthen writing issues throughout the revision process. As I shared my own first revision brainstorm, I expressed how my purpose for this writing project changed. While my first poem captured moments from my personal past, I realized I now wanted to find the essence of where I'm from while expressing who I am now. Because of this newly brainstormed purpose, my revision strategy was to start over altogether. I told my students that this is not always the appropriate revision strategy, but it was the right one for me in the context of my writing purpose. Students wanted to know if I restart often, and I told them that sometimes I do, but not all of the time.

For the second revision brainstorm, I focused on creating content. I tried to be as specific and poetic as possible, but I primarily paid attention to coming up with concrete details for each bubble and getting those details on paper. In the third revision brainstorm lesson, I demonstrated how I added poetic devices and language to my poem. I pointed to how I took the concrete details and revised those details to rework the language. The following is an excerpt from my third revision brainstorm. Included are sections from revision brainstorm two (in bold), and revisions that I made for brainstorm three (in italics).

Revision Brainstorm 3 (Adding Poetic Devices and Language)

Revision Note: This revision stage really was about cleaning up my language. I wanted to make it as close to the final draft as possible with a focus on poetic devices and poetic language. I tried to embellish the poetry with sensory details. I also looked up all the Asian words and spelled them correctly. I reworked many of the phrases, trying to add clarity and precision in this revision stage. I made lots of changes during this part of the revision process.

Bubble 1—Korean Roots

—Korean BBQ: **the salty play/twine of ginger root, garlic, and scallions**; *the salty twine of pungent ginger root, garlic, and green scallion ribbons nestled in a soy sauce marinade*

—Gyoza/Dumpling Wrapping: **manipulation of a wonton skin around mounds of pork and shrimp filling as the family works the gyoza at the kitchen table**; *manipulation of wonton skins around mounds of pork and shrimp filling, working the gyoza around the glass, kitchen table with my family*

—Korean War: **the fear, the hiding, the rations, the blare of bombs, and the crack of ammunition**; *stifling fear, dank caverns, gripped rations, blaring bombs, and the cracks of ammunition*

—Hato: **the slap of Pung and the hilarity of female talk**; *the slap of Pung and hilarity of feminine companionship*

I waited a few days before going over revision brainstorms four and five. During this time, I had students continue to write and revise while I conducted individual teacher-student conferences.

Revision brainstorm four involved finding and organizing meaning. I had to decide how I was going to organize my thoughts. I told my students that I looked at each bubble and at the poem as a whole. I decided to go from concrete to conceptual, starting with foods and ending with my philosophy. I showed my students how I moved the units around to come up with a specific order. Finally, I shared revision brainstorm five, the final step, which was putting everything together. I explained how I connected ideas and added transitional words or phrases to create flow. I also grouped units to add visual shape to the poem. After I read my final poem, the students applauded. I emphasized to them that the poem ended up the way it did because I went through the five revision brainstorm phases. Through my mentoring and modeling, students could trace my revision process from beginning to end. This process of adding and reworking translated well to their own poetry pages. Students embraced the revision process, and the success of the lesson astounded even me. The following is my final poetry mentor text that seemed to inspire my students:

Where I Am From

I am from the salty twine of pungent ginger root, garlic, and green scallion
    ribbons,
nestled in a soy sauce marinade and the manipulation of wonton skins
around mounds of pork and shrimp filling as my family works the gyoza
around the glass, kitchen table.

I am from jook, Chinese sausage, meat powder, and caramelized anchovies
and the billows of steam with simmering cabbage, tofu, and paper thin meat,
wafting upward from a shabu shabu skillet.

I am from the bright sheen of yellow daisies and floral shapes quilted in a
    fluffed, native futon;
the slap of Pung and hilarity of feminine companionship;
hakkyo, harmony, and kamsahamnida;
a 4.0;
stifling fear, dank caverns, gripped rations, blaring bombs, and the cracks of
    ammunition;
and the hover of ancestors long past.

I am from my familiars—my happiness, my family, my light;
the reliable presence of familial love;
and family in every facet of life.

I am from the act of teaching and the joyous pupils;
and the day to day routines:
the mundane and the common, everyday life.

I am from structuralism as the architect of the mind;
the elusive synthesis in dialectics;
Lawrence's grounding synthesis of physicality and spirituality;
Woolf's stream of consciousness and theoretical structure;
and Joyce—the visionary of language and thought.

I am from Wordsworth's lyrical . . . *Prelude* and the romantic Child;
Poe's coined minor poetry in "The Poetic Principle" and
the aesthetic cry of "Ligeia";
the Dickinsonian minor poem;
and "The Impercipient" and the poetic exile.

I am from my confessional voice; the poetic mode within my mind and
    heart;
my dreams where ideas percolate and come to fruition;
and my progression of predecessors' work in the artistic realm.

I am from the consciousness of a mind undone.
I am from the unconsciousness of a mind unknown.

—Dr. Frances Lin

Each student went through a similar revision process to produce a successful, final draft of their memoir poetry. And while many of the students' memoir poems captured the essence of my revision lessons, two left a special impression on me. First, my conference with a struggling student, Joel, who embraced this writing assignment, was especially rewarding. His initial poem was extremely short, but I noted that his unique ideas were a true strength of his writing. More descriptions and details were needed, but Joel said he was stuck. We rewrote a line together as I explained how I came up with some of my ideas. After a few revision lessons, Joel really caught on, and the second conference was all about combining ideas concisely and precisely. The end result was exciting for both Joel and me. He enjoyed his writing and threw himself into the memoir poem activities. The following is a before-and-after snapshot of a few of his lines:

Rough Draft

I am from dallas cowboys, inside zone
I am from love scars, you used to say you in love
I am from 44 more, Kevin Durant i'm a champion

Final Draft

I am from the Dallas Cowboys, inside zone, when the player breaks a
tackle runs up field dripping sweat while the energy pumps up his body
as he sees the endzone.

I am from bread, the fresh, soft smell of bread, the light brown crisp
color of French bread

I am from Allen Hurns, the wide receiver for the Dallas Cowboys,
when he hears the word "hike," and the play starts to move. He looks
the corner dead in the way to break him off and get open when he
reaches that 10-yard line. He plants his left foot to take a sharp right to
run his route, and the grass flies because the way his cleats dug into the
ground.

A second student, Joyce, had teacher-student conferences with me primarily
to discuss my last revision brainstorm lesson—putting everything together. She
wanted to know how I combined units with transitional phrases to develop a flow
throughout my final poem. Her writing sample exhibits how she transferred this
modeling into her own work. We also discussed one of my revision lessons about
adding sensory details and poetic language and devices to my memoir poem while
adding unique elements that express who I am. Joyce's writing sample reflects how
she did this herself to produce a final draft. Here are some sections of her rough
and final drafts:

Rough Draft

I am from family memories, eating crunchy shrimp and
chicken strips with ranch at Red Robin,
watching *Ringmaster* and *E.T.* while laughing and
crying at the same time,
studying hard for Science and Math Olympiad and
Academic Pentathlon, and celebrating my wins with a
Refreshing Starbuck's frappuccino.

Final Draft

I am from the state of Kerala, India, watching
Bangalore Days and Karinkkunnam 6's,
Contentedly eating soft, spicy egg puffs and
sweet, orange, spiraled jalebi,
and from the beautiful, unique flowers,
fresh with the morning dew, their
distinctive aromas filling the humid air.

All of my students saw how my initial poem was nothing like my final poem. This gave them the freedom to develop their words and to make changes that had a significant impact on their final creations. At the end of this poetry unit, most of my students were proud of their poems, and I was reminded of how effective and powerful mentoring and sharing is for young writers in a writing workshop approach.

Conclusion: Finding the Rewards of Effective Writing Instruction

My students learned so much during this process, and even I was surprised at the results. There was such a dramatic difference between the early and final drafts my students created. Student writers embraced the process of revision and emulated my modeling of the revision process using my own memoir poetry. Once students grasped the thought process I went through when revising the original poem, they were able to apply it to their own writing. They didn't simply use the thesaurus to make improvements. Instead, they thought carefully about how to approach revision using some of the strategies I demonstrated. Effective modeling and sharing was at the heart of this lesson. Although I had assigned the memoir poem quite a few times throughout the years, this was the first time I had included revision lessons based in process modeling. Students picked up on it and were able to revise with spirit.

Through the memoir poem, students discovered who they were and how their unique qualities can be understood by others to foster tolerance and understanding of different cultures, thoughts, and ideas about living. We built a community in our classroom through the sharing of authentic writing and by breaking down and modeling effective revision strategies. I was able to support my students as true writers as I conferred with them and discussed their work. This revision unit was successful, but it also marks the evolution of my writing instruction. Regardless of how much experience a veteran teacher has, there is always something around the corner that can improve and enhance writing experiences for young writers. My revision lessons have added an important dimension to my teaching of writing, and this unit brought an excitement to my teaching that I hadn't experienced in a long time. The class grew closer together because of this work. With genuine hope, I will continue sharing my teaching and personal writing journey with my students to help them enjoy writing too—for some of them, perhaps even for the first time.

Learning Tracker

As you read Frances's chapter, did you consider the ways you write alongside your students? What might that look like? As you spend class time on the difficult task of revision, what challenges do your students face? How might you help students see the value in revising their own work, as well as assisting their peers to revise their work? How can revising writing alongside your students better help them put their writing into the world? What is one takeaway you could implement within your teaching soon?

References

Bialosky, J. (2013, Spring). The unreasoning mask: The shared interior architecture of poetry and memoir. *Kenyon Review Online*. Retrieved from https://www.kenyonreview.org/kronline-issue/2013-spring/selections/jill-bialosky-656342/

Dorfman, L. R., & Cappelli, R. (2012). *Poetry mentor texts: Making reading and writing connections, K–8*. Portland, ME: Stenhouse Publishers.

Lyon, G. E. (1999). *Where I'm from*. Retrieved from http://www.georgeellalyon.com/where.html

National Council of Teachers of English. (2016). *Professional knowledge for the teaching of writing*. Urbana, IL: Author. Retrieved from http://www2.ncte.org/statement/teaching-writing/

Sommers, N. (1980). Revision strategies of student writers and experienced adult writers. *College Composition and Communication*, *31*(4), 378–88. http://dx.doi.org/10.2307/356588

Witte, S. (2013). Preaching what we practice: A study of revision. *Journal of Curriculum and Instruction*, *6*(2), 33–59.

The Classroom That Inquiry Built: Student- and Purpose-Driven Literacy Learning

Sarah Bonner
Heyworth Junior High School, Heyworth, IL

Straight from a Norman Rockwell painting, my small, rural school district in Illinois provides for about 400 students in grades 7–12. What my district may not have in diversity or resources it makes up for in heart for its students and schools. And, while my district ranges in socioeconomic level, the developmental characteristics of teenagers still hold true for any middle grades educator. Within my small school, my classroom is the one that inquiry built. As the result of a student-driven design initiative connected to an inquiry-based study several years ago, my classroom showcases one of the more unique learning environments in our building. It offers a variety of seating with movable tables, rolling office chairs, stools, and comfort seating in a reading area lovingly called "the den."

In addition to my classroom's unique physical design, my students operate in a "no-grades" classroom throughout the entire year. After implementing and facilitating my first Genius Hour five years ago, I approached a crossroads in my assessment practices. Given the basic elements underlying this unit (i.e., inquiry, personalized learning experiences, and student interaction with civic engagement concepts), I noticed that my assessments no longer seemed to fit the classroom learning goals. Applying a numeric value to student passion seemed disconnected from the student learning experience. The moment I attached a number grade and rubric to our Genius Hour, I turned an extensive, passion-driven learning journey into "just a project." In fact, it became an ongoing joke in our classroom throughout my first year of implementing Genius Hour. Specifically, I recall a student saying to me, "Mrs. Bonner, you mean my passion is only worth 50 points?! I feel like that's so cheap!" Agreeing wholeheartedly, I ventured into an assessment overhaul by examining the idea of going gradeless in an effort to support my new view on teaching and learning with inquiry.

As a result of going gradeless, student assessment now focuses on participation, progress, and performance in students' literacy journey by utilizing narrative reflection; continuous feedback, from both peers and myself; and grade negotiation conferences. When students become empowered to lead their own learning, they need facilitation, scaffolding, resources, accountability, and encouragement. Genius Hour not only fosters student empowerment, but it also supports a wide range of learning standards. In addition to participation, progress, and performance, this inquiry experience enables students to demonstrate their understanding of reading, writing, speaking, listening, and language skills.

While reading and writing may be designated times throughout the school day according to student schedules, the design of the class integrates both reading and writing practices together. My classroom thrives in student interest, facilitation, peer support, collaboration, and inquiry. It is this mindset that allows Genius Hour to become one of the more impactful moments throughout the year for my language arts students.

Writing as Inquiry through Genius Hour

Genius Hour (or 20% Time)—originating from Google's policy allowing engineers to use 20 percent of their work week to explore pet projects connected to bettering the company—translates into the classroom in a similar manner. Under the Genius Hour framework, students design passion-based, personalized inquiry projects with civic engagement threads to be worked on one day a week for a specified amount of time. While many schools have integrated Genius Hour into their classrooms, many teachers are hesitant to give up one day a week for a student-driven inquiry project.

Even though many traditional English language arts classrooms engage in topics relevant to our world through literature and writing prompts, they rarely promote the physical act of service and activism. With its connections to long-lasting civic engagement and vast array of literacy standards, Genius Hour offers a path to think about how ELA teachers can create learning experiences that empower student voices and give students opportunities to write for audiences beyond the classroom.

As I approached my tenth year of teaching, I realized that I wanted to evolve my practice. While I felt that the curriculum I had designed and implemented for many years seemed engaging and purposeful, I found myself wanting more. I remember feeling an inner struggle between the teacher I was and the teacher I wanted to become. The teacher I was showed strength, demonstrated strong content knowledge, and had put many effective practices in place. Needless to say, that side of me was comfortable in my teaching skin. However, this comfort became unsettling, and I began to believe I needed to change my practice to embody more student advocacy, interest-based learning, and technology integration, especially since our district became a 1:1 Chromebook school that particular year.

Upon reflection, I concluded that the ELA classroom supports a conceptual freedom that other content area classrooms do not. As I gave myself permission to think beyond the literary canon, I started to research inquiry-based methods in an effort to seek change—especially since the nature of Genius Hour allows classrooms to integrate this model one day a week. Implementing Genius Hour into my ELA classroom challenged my poses as an educator and allowed me to understand that I can have a dynamic influence on empowering my students.

Genius Hour not only afforded me the opportunity to strengthen student engagement through tapping into their personal interests, but it also allowed me to be a copilot in student learning experiences that fostered personalization, passion, and action. Playing to these strengths changed my outlook on teaching. Breaking away from the traditional images and procedures of school enabled me to pave a new path for my students. Spencer and Juliani (2017) describe the Genius Hour experience as a means to empower students to organically seek out learning opportunities and construct authentic demonstration of that learning. Throughout the quest to empower students through the 20% Time (or Genius Hour) model, Spencer and Juliani also recognize that this process highlights the unknown. As a veteran teacher venturing into this new territory, I understood very quickly that my power dynamic within the classroom demanded change, and I had to accept that learning should be a mutual conversation rather than a dictation of knowledge. Genius Hour redefined my role as teacher into more of a facilitator. Students situated themselves as the expert in their own learning in connection to personalized topics.

For my students, Genius Hour became a vessel that transformed the way they viewed reading, writing, and learning. The nature of this inquiry-based design encourages discovery through reading and writing, but the purpose of those activities changes as the project becomes more than "just an assignment." Students invested in their learning journey because it allowed them the freedom to explore their own passions. If we know that the road to finding one's passion is not a straight line, then it's essential that students participate in learning that can ultimately impact potential future actions and decisions. My students are not ignorant about the issues the world currently faces; therefore, they are continuously looking for opportunities to create awareness, promote a cause, engage in conversation, and try on new identities so that they can better read the world (Friere & Macedo, 1987).

Professional Knowledge for the Teaching of Writing

Two of the foundational principles of NCTE's *Professional Knowledge for the Teaching of Writing* (PKTW) position statement (2016) offer critical perspectives on my use of Genius Hour.

"Writing grows out of many purposes."

While the appeal of incorporating Genius Hour into the ELA classroom connects to multiple facets of literacy learning standards, Genius Hour heavily interacts with the writing process given the amount of communication needed throughout the stages of inquiry. According to the PKTW, "Writing with certain purposes in mind, the writer focuses attention on what the audience is thinking or believing; other times, the writer focuses more on the information she or he is organizing, or on her or his own emergent thoughts and feelings" (p. ix). As the stages of Genius Hour unfold, students use writing as a platform to ignite, organize, inform, and act upon topics that speak readily to their interests and passions. Due to Genius Hour's focus on interest-based learning, student writing becomes an intrinsic necessity rather than a formulaic chore.

As ELA teachers consider the direction of writing instruction in their own classrooms, Genius Hour permits a variety of writing activities connected to personalized topics, which strengthens student agency in relation to various types of writing. Within my own classroom, students begin the Genius Hour process by drafting a series of personal narratives through journal prompts in an effort to ignite the foundational question, "What am I passionate about?" Once students explore their own interests and potential passions, writing then becomes a means to explore the facets of a specific topic. As a writing teacher who uses learning standards as a road map to learning goals, I can readily incorporate narrative, informational, and argumentative writing activities into the curriculum; but Genius Hour requires students to manipulate those genres of writing in practical formats. From op-eds to proposals for the local city council meeting, writing for a great purpose takes a strong hold of students throughout this process.

"Writing is a tool for thinking."

In addition to writing for various purposes, Genius Hour lends itself to writers as an opportunity to use writing as a means to process thought. The PKTW states that writing is used "to solve problems, to identify issues, to construct questions, to reconsider something one had already figured out, to try out a half-baked idea" (p. xix). One of the primary components of introducing and implementing a solid foundation for my Genius Hour structure relates to the idea of addressing a need and matching that with personal passion. To my students, filling this need might be explicitly personal; but it could also be bigger than themselves: it could impact their families, school environment, community, or local area. To think through concepts that promote creating awareness, invite change, or support innovation requires a platform from which to process ideas. For my students, writing became that platform in their efforts to forge ahead with pursuing their passions; it also contributed greatly to empowering their voices as individuals.

Writing Instruction and Position Statement Connections

To illustrate Genius Hour in an ELA classroom, I want to highlight a student who participated in this inquiry-based writing experience and agreed to share his work. In addition to showcasing his work, I reflect on the stages of student writing and how my role as a writing teacher impacts the writer's experience.

Caleb, an energetic fourteen-year-old, approached me at the beginning of our Genius Hour journey to tell me about the conversation he and his dad had about choosing a potential project. Seeing his older brother participate in Genius Hour two years prior and spending a significant amount of time on our community's baseball fields, Caleb wanted to design a project that would have a positive impact on our environment. Throughout the first stage of writing in his journey through inquiry, Caleb drafted personal narratives that related to many of his baseball games and how the mosquitos

Stage 1: Getting Started Personal Narratives, Journal Exercises, Outlining General Research, Introducing Supportive Writing Material

in the summer months can be almost unbearable. With this initial drafting, Caleb realized very quickly that he had discovered a potential problem with a need for a solution. Through his beginning writings, research skimming, and the influence of his father, Caleb concluded that he wanted to study bat boxes, their positive effects on the environment, and how these positive effects could benefit his community.

Because I wasn't familiar with the topic of bat boxes, I knew I needed to support Caleb in achieving a direction he would be comfortable moving toward as he ventured deeper into his project. Giving myself permission to not be the "expert" in everything allowed me to focus on my expertise in writing, questioning, guiding, and brainstorming. It became clear that I needed to support Caleb by asking deep questions that would encourage him to think critically about this topic. In addition, I gave Caleb the time he needed to process these thoughts through his own personal narratives and conversations with his family. All of these factors contributed to the development of his inquiry project and inspired the next steps of research, as well as activism.

Once Caleb felt comfortable with his chosen topic through the assistance of brainstorming and personal narrative prompt writing, he began to formulate the details of his project. Up until now, Caleb had relied on a familiar type of writing—a narrative, story-like genre that showcased personal experience. Once he decided to focus on bat boxes, Caleb's writing switched to posing real questions, creating a pitching concept for others to view and provide feedback, and utilizing an outline that would help guide and shape his study.

Stage 2: Formulating the Project
Generating Questions, Pitching Concepts to Others, Obtaining Feedback, Drafting Outlines to Begin the Shape of the Project

Because formulating Caleb's project relied heavily not only on articulating the project itself, but also on the need for feedback and buy-in from others, I wanted to make sure that Caleb had an audience larger than just his peers. In addition to having previous students visit our classroom to give my current students verbal feedback, I encouraged Caleb and his peers to start their own blogs, which allowed them to document their learning journeys, and also lent agency to their writing. Caleb's personal blog space served not only as a platform for conceptualizing his project, but also as a means to interact with various readers through his writing.

After formulating his specific questions and research, Caleb worked to become an expert on his topic. From personal narrative to outlining, brainstorming, and sketching potential plans, Caleb's writing purpose changed once again as he thought about what it meant to be an expert at something. Caleb's informational writing in his blog (see Appendix A) will look familiar to many ELA teachers who assign this kind of writing, but for Caleb, this specific informational piece of writing was intrinsically motivating and served a greater purpose beyond any prompt or rubric of the traditional writing classroom.

Stage 3: Becoming the Expert
Specific Research and Informative Writing, Interviewing Mentor(s) for Support

This stage of the Genius Hour project, becoming an expert, feels urgent to students, so I wanted to ensure that Caleb's writing supported him in achieving this goal. In addition to more traditional practices that writing teachers assign when working through an informational writing unit, I also required Caleb to network with a mentor in connection with his specific topic. And, while this may sound easy, don't assume that students today can make these contacts successfully and independently. So, on top of formulating a piece of informational research writing through his blog, Caleb also wrote a series of emails that might allow him to network with others who could speak to his interest in bringing bat boxes to our community. Although this step wasn't necessary for all writers in my class, it was a great learning opportunity for Caleb and enhanced his ownership of his writing as I used scaffolding strategies and feedback to support his writing goals.

The ebb and flow of inquiry allowed Caleb to revisit his initial questioning about bat boxes as well as his personal narratives related to mosquitos, playing baseball, and attempting to solve a problem at the community park. While Caleb tinkered with several ideas, including the physical construction of a bat box, we also considered how writing might be a powerful resource if developed into a proposal for our local city council. As Caleb's inquiry came to this cross-roads—did he want to build a bat box to be placed in the park or write a proposal for our community local government?—his project evolved into an impactful discussion about the power of writing. Caleb and I discussed options for engaging in problem solving, but the more we spoke on this topic, the more he and I realized that gaining the support of local officials would bring a heightened level of awareness to his cause. Ultimately, Caleb drafted a proposal to be submitted and presented at a town hall meeting (see Appendix B).

> **Stage 4: Activism & Engagement**
> Creating Products That Connect to Engagement (media products, etc.).

We often think of inquiry as being appropriate only for science or other content area classrooms, but there's no reason it can't be implemented in ELA classrooms to create positive change through writing. Caleb's work—as well as other students' work throughout the years—provides an outlook on writing that I would never have been able to obtain had I not taken the risk to implement Genius Hour in my classroom. While Caleb's proposal still sits at city hall (politics as usual), it represents a victory in student writing because it not only reinforces the empowerment of student voices like Caleb's, but it also confirms the responsibility I have as a writing teacher to cultivate learning experiences that spark positive change.

Conclusion: Learning to Learn

Holland and colleagues (2001) address identity and the formation of identity through a figured world framework. Essentially, people assimilate their identities through their actions, influences, and specific communities. Holland et al. state that a person's figured world envelops traditions and surroundings that contribute to the development of the individual's "truth." My students live in a small community and understand their "truth" to be only what they have always known. Their figured world encompasses only a small facet of the multitudes that constitute the larger world. Our students' narrow perspective plays to our strengths as teachers because they are authentically asking questions that seek to expand their truth.

In addition, my students know how to "play school." Throughout their years as students, they have become conditioned to the traditional practices of school. They find comfort in them and periodically complain, "Can't we just have the worksheet?" Genius Hour allows them to understand true *learning*. Not only were students exposed to and experience different genres of writing depending on their personalized inquiries, but they also cultivated experiences in unwritten skills such as perseverance, tenacity, making connections and relationships, and occasionally failing. They also learned that their voices and actions can create positive change in our school and community climate and culture. For Caleb, writing seemed formulaic and distant before his Genius Hour experience, as if it were another box to check as he ground through the motions of school. And, while he might argue that some of his blog posts felt like writing-as-usual, he eventually understood that writing plays a significant role in planning, becoming an expert, communicating, and fostering change.

As for my experience, I want to give other ELA teachers permission to think about how inquiry can make a lasting impact on both student literacy and student empowerment. I understand the rigor, the pressure, and the pushback of maintaining the status quo and ensuring that literacy learning standards are continuously being met within the classroom . . . but why should literacy learning continue to look the way it always has? Think about Caleb's Genius Hour experience, the partnership writing and civic engagement he had with others throughout the project. And remember, Genius Hour takes just 20 percent of standard class time, making room for a blending of traditional and innovative pedagogy.

Genius Hour changed my view of teaching and learning after having taught middle school for fifteen years. This experience allows students to choose a topic that speaks to their curiosities, as well as promotes student empowerment. Youth-driven inquiry projects aren't common in our small district because they move beyond the traditional classroom, but I learned that school doesn't have to look like that. If we want our students to be active participants in the world, we have a moral calling to create learning experiences that nurture and foster avenues for students to develop their own voices so that they too can see and be the change they want.

Learning Tracker

As you read Sarah's chapter, did you consider how you might make time for student-driven inquiry projects in your classroom? How does inquiry provide motivation and engagement for students? How would a no-grades approach to teaching writing be implemented in your classroom or school? What opportunities do you provide for students to enter or impact the world with their work? What is one takeaway you could implement within your teaching soon?

Appendix A: Caleb's Informational Blog on Bat Boxes

Introduction

Bat boxes are a great way to solve many problems, and can help your overall park experience. A bat box is a box that can be hung on a tree/house in order to house bats. Implementing bat boxes into the community is good for the community for a variety of reasons. These include bug population, pollination, and guano(poop).

Why Are Bat Boxes Important

Bats and bat boxes are important for various reasons. One reason bats are important is cutting the bug population. By adding bats into the environment, the bug population will go down significantly. Guano (bat poop) makes great fertilizer and helps things grow, this guano can also contain seeds and create a new plant. Bats are also pollinators, many plants rely on them. Bats are also important for the wellbeing of the community. You will read about these things later on in this blog.

Bug Population

By implementing bats into an enviroment, the bug population will decrease significantly. According to the national parks service, bats feast on insects each night and add up to 3.7 billion dollars worth of pest control in the U.S. With bats eating

bugs, it actually helps farmers. With the bugs gone, there a fewer insects causing damage to crops. This saves the farmers money by making them not spend as much on pest control. Since the town of heyworth has fields all around it, I believe this would be greatly beneficial for the whole community. This is one way bats can impact an enviroment in a positive way.

Guano

Guano is another word for bat poop. Now it may not seem like this substance would be able to do anything for the enviroment, but it actually can. Guano makes amazing fertilizer and may carry fruit seeds. By these seeds going into the ground with a good fertilizer, fruit trees/bushes will be able to grow and produce. This is of course good and fruit picking makes for a good healthy activity to do in spare time.

Bat Box Hanging

Hanging a bat box may not be as simple as it seems. Most people would think "Oh just find a nice tree and nail it up", when there is a little more that goes into it. The first step in hanging a bat box is making sure you have the right color bat box. If the box stands out, predators will easily see it and eat all the bats. A good color for a bat box to be in Illinois is a dark brown or a grey. This way the bat will still see it as their home, but predators will not easily find it. The next step is actually

hanging the box. As I said earlier you can't just nail it to a tree. The needs to be 15-20 ft. of air space between the box and the ground for the bats to be able to leave correctly. They need time to open their wings and begin their flight once they drop out of their box. This space will also stop any unwanted fiddling with the boxes from any curious child. As you can see, hanging a bat box can be a little more complex than you think.

Action Plan

There are multiple steps to making this idea become a reality. The first step for me is finding a mentor. I have contacted 2 people but neither agreed to be my mentor. The next step is asking Town Hall for permission to hang bat boxes at the park. I am currently formulating a letter to ask for permission and hopefully they will tell me I can do my idea. The third step is of course getting my hand on a bat box. My idea for this is reaching out to a company and see if I can get them to donate, and if not I may have to dip into my own funds to buy bat boxes. The next step would be to hang up my newly acquired bat box. As I talked about earlier I will have to do all the things to make sure The box is successful. Bats should filter into the box on their own once it is hung up. The last thing to do is to look at how much my idea is helping the community. These are the steps I will have to take in order for my project to become a success.

Goal

My goal for this project is to hang bat boxes at our Centennial Park and have it affect the community in a positive way. I also want to inform others about the importance of bats and bat boxes. I will have to overcome a few obstacles along the way, but I believe the end goal is worth it.

Conclusion

I hope many good things come from this idea. I hope I am able to do something good for my community. I hope I can impact the lives of people around me. Lastly, I hope to make Centennial Park a better and more enjoyable place for everyone.

Appendix B: Caleb's Town Hall Proposal Writing (Draft)

Bat Boxes

In my language arts class, we are doing a Genius Hour project. Genius Hour is a project in which students choose a topic to further learn about. I have chosen bat boxes, and wants to help the community.

Goal

My overarching goal for this project to to help the community of Heyworth. From the research I have learned, bat boxes are a great way to positively impact you town and environment.

Specific Goals

- Hang bat boxes up at Centennial Park
- Cut down on the pesky Bug Population
- Possibly start new plant life

The Problem

I feel like there is an annoying problem going on at Centennial park. This problem is the amount of bugs. I as a baseball player, am out there fairly often. During practices and work times, I feel like bugs can get in the way of my performance. I'm sure other people feel the exact same way about this. I am looking to solve this problem for me and my community,

Solution

My solution for this problem it to hang bat boxes at the park. Bat boxes would contain bats and the bats would fly around eating bugs and making the park a more comfortable place.

Cost

I have been contacting some bat box manufacturers to try to get a donation of a bat box. Not yet have I gotten a response, but I still have high hopes.

Research

I have gathered some information about this topic I would like to share. The first good thing bats do is eat bugs and cut down drastically on the bug population. Another good things bats do is spread their guano. Bats guano is filled with good fertilizer and plant seeds. This would help plants grow, and possibly start new plant life. Bats are also great pollinators, helping plants reproduce. This is what I have learned about my subject, and I believe it can help the community.

References

Freire, P., & Macedo, D. (1987). *Literacy: Reading the word and the world.* Westport, CT: Bergin and Garvey.

Holland, D. C., Lachicotte, Jr., W. S., Skinner, D., & Cain, C. (2001). *Identity and agency in cultural worlds.* Cambridge, MA: Harvard University Press.

National Council of Teachers of English. (2016). *Professional knowledge for the teaching of writing.* Retrieved from http://www.ncte.org/positions/statements/teaching-writing

Spencer, J., & Juliani, A. J. (2017). *Empower: What happens when students own their learning.* IMPress.

Part II
Writing That Moves the World

In this section, we highlight two different approaches to writing instruction that allows students to write in ways that move, or shift, their worldviews and experiences. From the micro perspective of reading and modeling poetry, Tracei motivates her students with mentor texts to build their writing confidence. Through the shared experience of writing poetry coupled with frank discussions of social issues, students take ownership of their literacy lives. From a macro perspective, Margaret implements problem-based learning to gamify her curriculum. Her middle level kids design games for younger learners and, in the process, expand the idea of "purpose" through creatively approaching their own learning with others in mind. These teachers and students use the power of writing to motivate, investigate, and interrogate their understandings of the world.

Learning Tracker

As you read Part II, *Writing That Moves the World*, consider how reading and writing are connected in your class-room. Whose stories are being written and shared in your classroom? Whose stories are being left out? How do you include the topics students care about in your curriculum? How relevant is your curriculum to the lives your students lead? In what ways do you help your students understand the power of the written word in the world?

That's My Kind of Magic: Writing to Build Community with Middle Level Kids

Tracei Willis
Louisville High School, Louisville, MS

My Magic

Sometimes,
when the words are flowing just right,
and my pencil is going
scratcha-scratcha-squeak-squeak
across the page of my journal . . .
It's like magic.

Like the words are blazing a fire through me
and I have to get them out
or they will consume me . . .
that's some raging magic.

When I've had a poem
Creeping about in my head
for days and days,
and it's wormed its way up
through my soul
making its way down my arm
tingling into my hand,
and onto that page . . .

man,
that's my magic.

When I share those words,
and those words take on a life
in the eyes of another . . .
it becomes our magic.

A "it's me plus you
and together we can
be just right" kinda magic.

Simple and true,
no potions or spells,
just letters
forming words
forming lines
forming poems
Transforming minds . . .
prolific & poetic,
That's my kind of magic.
—Tracei Willis (2016)

"Do you believe in magic?" That was the journal prompt I gave my eighth graders the day I scribbled a messy draft of "My Magic" into my writing journal, but I was introduced to the magic of poetry when I was twelve years old. My mom worked cooking and cleaning for many of the mighty fine families on Tally Ho Drive, and one particular matron gifted me a copy of Nikki Giovanni's Cotton Candy on a Rainy Day. *It was at that point in my life that I realized the power of poetry. No, I didn't know in that moment that Nikki Giovanni had changed not only my life but also my worldview—that would come much later with much reflection on the day Helen Mullen handed me a book of poetry written by a woman who looked like me.*

Just before school was out this year, my principal stopped me on my way back from the cafeteria. Looking very stern, he said he wanted to ask me a question, and I wondered what form I had neglected to fill out. . . .

Mr. Hudson said, "Everywhere I look, my ninth graders are reading. In the auditorium in the morning, in the office, everywhere I look, a freshman has a book—how are you doing this? How are you getting them to read?"

His question made me smile; actually, I smiled to suppress a laugh. I didn't have time to go into detail about research and the power of finding each student's personal Nikki Giovanni, so I just told him, "I got to know the kids and then helped them make a connection with a book; no big deal."

Each new school year I walk into my classroom a few weeks before school starts, I stare at boxes that need to be unpacked, I sit in the dark, and I reflect on the year before: *What worked? What didn't work? Who am I now? What kind of students will enter this room in a few weeks? Will they love to read and write as much as I do? Will they hate to read and write? Will I be able to reach them all?* This chapter provides a glimpse into the ways our classroom builds community and writing fluency through the shared reading and writing of poetry.

Professional Knowledge for the Teaching of Writing

Two particular elements in NCTE's *Professional Knowledge for the Teaching of Writing* position statement (2016) offer critical perspectives on my use of reading and writing poetry with my students.

"Writing and reading are related."

I believe that to be a good writer, students need to be hungry readers. By hungry readers, I mean consuming books as though they can't get enough of them. I use authors' texts as examples of excellent writing, and I always emphasize what I like about the moves the author has made and the ways the author makes their mark on the world. My classroom is not "rich," but it is "text rich." It is filled with donated books, purchased books, library books, begged and borrowed books . . . all the ways I can get books in the hands of my students.

"Conventions of finished and edited texts are an important dimension of the relationship between writers and readers."

Grammar, spelling, sentence structure, and punctuation are all important factors in reading and writing. It makes my eyes water when I'm reading a meme or a social media post in which someone used *your* instead of *you're* or *than* instead of *then*—but I don't confront those people and call them out. Likewise, in the beginning of the school year, I don't blast my students' writing with grammar and spelling corrections, because I don't want them to lose their voice or to see me only as an editor. When it comes to student writing, I read it first as a reader. I read their writing looking strictly for what they did well. Do my students misspell words? Misuse words? Write like they text? Write using slang? Misplace commas and forget to use end marks? Of course they do. But it's more important to me that they know I value foremost what they have to say.

Early on I introduce my students to Don and Jenny Killgallon's "Imitating the Grammar of the Greats" (2006), and from day one we examine sentences taken from award-winning novels. We examine a sentence each day just to see what the writer did well; what the sentence helps us to see, taste, hear, smell, or feel; and what we don't understand about the sentence. After several weeks of examining sentences, we learn to break them down into meaningful chunks, and one section at a time we start to imitate the style and structure of these sentences using our own content.

Over the course of the school year, we examine the way writers use adjectives and adverbs and look at their placement within the sentence, such as opening with adjectives or adverbs versus delayed adjectives or adverbs. We also learn to use six different types of phrases by examining the way published writers use them—one sentence at a time. And for every word, phrase, clause, paragraph, poem, or essay I ask my students to write, I write right alongside them, mistakes and all. I think it helps students to see me go through revisions, to see that first drafts are called "rough" for a reason.

Reading the Classroom

On our first day together, I ask my students to "read the classroom," to walk around and make observations, and through those observations, to make three inferences about me. To decide what kind of teacher I will be. To figure out what kind of expectations I have for them. To see if they have anything in common with me. Usually their responses go something like this:

> You want us to be kind to one another.
>
> You really like books.
>
> You really like quotes from books.
>
> You like to write.
>
> You like people who write books.
>
> You expect us to read books.
>
> You like poetry.
>
> You're going to expect us to write a lot.
>
> You like *Doctor Who*.

They are not wrong. I am all those things and more. Our classroom is print-rich—from book quotes to song lyrics, from comic strips to *Doctor Who* quotes, our walls are worth reading. Some of my students might even consider me to be a bit overly enthusiastic about reading and writing. Seriously, a few have looked me up on Facebook and reported back that every other post is about a book I just finished reading or a poem I just wrote. But my students? Not so much enthusiasm for reading and writing. Most come to me having never read a book from cover to cover; some have no desire to read a book, while others have never had the opportunity to choose their own books. They've been exposed to test-prep passages, computer-based reading programs, and reading skills notes on novels read as a class, but not many have been asked to truly connect with characters that look like them, talk like them, and face situations like theirs. The first battle we face is the "But Miss, I don't like to read" battle.

I make sure students understand that they can put a book down if they don't understand it or just don't like it. I designate class time for reading because I believe if we ask students to read independently but don't give them time to do so, we are setting them up to fail. I want to see their faces as they fall in love with characters and to engage them in conversations about what they are reading. I encourage them to talk to one another after independent reading by asking them to mix and mingle and share with at least three other students why their book is worth reading. Then as a whole group we come back together to share who is reading something we want to read. I include myself in the mix and mingle because I want them to know that I'm a reader too. I am not asking them to do something that I am not willing to do.

Within the first week of school, students are being connected with books in our classroom library. I'm being greeted at the door by previously self-proclaimed "nonreaders" who are upset with me over the way a book ended. I'm watching as unexpected laughter catches a student off guard because she read something funny in her book. I've seen tears fall involuntarily during independent reading, and I've seen students compete with one another to get from the seventh floor to the lobby of Jason Reynolds's *Long Way Down*, saying things to each other like "What floor are you on?" and "I already passed you!" Students making literary connections and complaining when the timer signals the end of independent reading time? I'm definitely calling it a win.

Engaged Readers Become Engaged Writers

Once my students accept their role as readers, they realize they also have stories to tell, but convincing students of their natural ability to write is an entirely different hard-fought battle than the battle about reading. My students come to their first writing conferences with me as though they're bringing their writing to a sacrificial altar to be burned by a fiery red pen. They come with criticism for their own writing, wanting me to tell them how to "fix" it. First, they need to understand that their writing is not broken, that whatever apprehension they are feeling about their words is the way most other writers feel too. Writing is hard, but we all have a story to tell, and we have to start somewhere. I need my students to understand that no matter what happens in our writing conference, they are the ones in control of their writing, their message, their truth.

I start by asking students to read their writing to me. I want them to take ownership of their writing. Then I point out the strongest words, phrases, or lines in their writing—these are usually the places where they have been the most honest and natural with their word choice. Next, I ask questions about words, phrases, or lines I don't understand, and I ask them to simply explain what they meant and consider writing it the way they explained it. I resist the natural urge to correct spelling and grammar usage because during writing conferences I need my students to accept themselves as writers who are responsible for communicating a message to the world. Each student has a message, a story, a truth to tell in their own voice using their own language. It is my responsibility to listen and guide, but ultimately to help them develop their own voice as a writer. But in the beginning, they seem defeated before we can even discuss their writing.

> So we start small.
> We start with poetry.
> Poetry holds the power to let students be heard.
> Poetry has the magic to show students they are writers.
> Poetry shouts loud and clear, your voice matters.

Most of my students believe in their hearts that they hate poetry. They've been exposed to some fancy, unrelatable poetry and they were probably asked to analyze said fancy, unrelatable poetry for a grade. So the first hurdle is to make poetry relatable.

We begin with the story of our names, reading excerpts from *Locomotion* by Jacqueline Woodson, a book written in verse about a boy named Lonnie who is living in foster care. We read Sandra Cisneros's vignette "My Name" from *The House on Mango Street* and Marge Piercy's "If I Had Been Called Sabrina or Ann, She Said," and listen to Uzo Aduba's testimonial about how she never liked her name. My students and I use these mentor texts as a starting point to tell the stories of our own names. We move from names to the people who raised us when we read the poem "Raised by Women" by Kelly Norman Ellis, and then on to the places we call home and the people who live there by reading "Where I'm From" by George Ella Lyons. I have been using Linda Christensen's *Reading, Writing, and Rising Up* (2000) as a guide for many years now to honor my students and their names through poetry. One very important thing has happened to me by starting the school year writing about our names—I remember students' names and they remember one another's names, because once you know the story behind someone's name, it's harder to forget; we know one another's stories and we are kinder to one another when we can see the human story in another person.

First Nine Weeks: And THEN We Write . . .

I spend the first nine weeks getting to know my students through their writing. They spend the first nine weeks reading relatable poetry and writing poetry about themselves. They also get to know and accept one another through the sharing of their writing. We have what I like to call Sacred Reading Time, Sacred Writing Time, and Sacred Sharing Time. Although I really enjoy all three, my favorite is Sacred Sharing Time. What's sacred about it? It's our time to spend with one another. It's our time to be present with one another, and we can share without fear of judgment. During Sacred Sharing Time, my students and I have laughed together, cried together, and sat in awe of the spoken word together. And what is so profound about this time is this—no matter how any of us feels after hearing what someone else shares, there is only one acceptable response:

"Thank you for sharing."

That's it.

No analysis.

No rebuttal.

No high praise.

No low praise.

Just "Thank you for sharing."

Through this process, my students hear one another and see one another in their most fragile states; they see one another as vulnerable human beings. And as a side bonus, they began to see poetry as a tool. A tool that can be used to forge social change.

One of my favorite poetic methods comes from Christensen's book *Reading, Writing, and Rising Up* (2000) called the "Write That I . . ." poem. We use this format during the first nine weeks to write about ourselves. Students respond to a series of journal questions: "What do you want your teachers to write about you after you graduate from high school?" or "What do you want your parents to write about you after you leave home?" or "What would you want a reporter to write about you if you died in an accident?" I share a "Write That I . . ." poem that I wrote for my daughters expressing what I would want them to say about me after I'm gone. I've found that my students really want to be remembered in a positive light, and not for their mistakes.

Brayam demonstrates this in his "Write That I . . ." poem:

Write that I always asked
"How was your day at school?"
that I always asked if you needed
help with anything.
Tell them I was always there for you,
through the good times and the bad.

Don't tell them that I lied sometimes.
Don't say that your mom doesn't like me
because of my big mouth.

Don't tell them we still saw each other
even though we weren't supposed to.
Don't tell them how mad I got when
You told me to run just so your parents
wouldn't see me . . .

Tell them that I was a loving and caring person—

Say that I was Brayam Munoz

We also read Lucille Clifton's poem "What the Mirror Said" and consider whether our mirrors lift us up or tear us down. We write about what our reflections say to us and how that self-talk affects the way we step out of our homes each morning. Their responses to this poem help me to see how my students see themselves and their place in this world.

Second Nine Weeks: Discovering Self with Difficult Conversations

My students spend the first nine weeks getting to know one another through their writing, but during the second nine weeks, I like to think they turn the lens inward and begin to look inside themselves to ask the piercing question, "What do I believe?"

Not, what does society believe?
Not, what do my parents believe?
Not, what do my classmates believe?
But what do I as an individual believe?
How do I get my students to ask that question?

We make lists of our beliefs, and then we make lists about what we question about our beliefs, and as a self-reflection tool, we fill our journals with quick-writes about topics on our lists. And then through poetry, of course, we set out to find ourselves in our writing. We start by reading "What I Believe" by Jacqueline Woodson, where we see that sometimes we might have beliefs that contradict each other, and that is okay too. Jada wrote her poem with this in mind.

Believe
Inspired by Jacqueline Woodson's "What I Believe"

I believe in having patience and cursing others out.
I believe in "Put a Praise on It" and "Set It Off"
I believe in speaking up and staying silent.
I believe in the wisdom of my grandmother.
I believe in the United States and Iraq.
I believe everything happens for a reason.
I believe in death and life.
I believe in my friend's bright skin and my dark complexion.
I believe in my sister's discombobulated plays and my easy routines.
I believe in my mother's kindness and people taking it for granted.

I believe in crazy friends and bizarre foods.
I believe in jaxs and hopscotch, the principals and students, iPhones and books,
    sober and drunk.
I believe in humanity.

I believe that one day and every day will come to an end.

—Jada Eichelberger

It's during the second nine weeks, after we've developed a culture of personal writing and expression, that we really start to have the difficult conversations. And how do we start the difficult conversations? Again, with poetry. This year I used a poem by Clint Smith called "How to Make a Cardboard Box Disappear in 10 Steps," a list poem that, in ten short lines, references the deaths of people of color who were shot and killed. My students then discussed the structure and format of the poem (without prompting) and immediately asked, "Is this even a poem?" and "I've never seen a poem like this before!"

I sat back and watched and thought, "Dang, is this what y'all get from this poem? Structure and format?" But then the conversation shifted as my students wondered who some of the people in the poem were—and they moved smoothly into the research phase. I divided them into groups to find out more information about the people mentioned in Smith's poem and asked them to write a group "Write That I . . ." poem to express what they discovered about the person they were researching. They found difficult answers, and some questions were left unanswered. One student commented on the last line of Smith's poem, saying that the blank line was unsettling and that she felt as though her name might fill that blank next.

Remember Me

Inspired by Clint Smith's "How to Make a Cardboard Box
Disappear in 10 Steps"

Write that I was 17 Years Old
Say that I was walking home
From the store
And that a snack and a hoodie
Cost me my life
Tell them I was just trying to get back home

Don't write that I was suspended
Don't say that I was just a thug
Who was just looking for trouble
Don't tell them I was just a druggie
Who deserved to be shot

Write that I was in Honors English
And that I was unarmed
Tell them I still had dreams
Say that I was Trayvon Martin

—Group One, 1st Block

We read Smith's poem as an introduction to reading *The Hate U Give* by Angie
Thomas, and many of our Socratic seminar sessions led back to that blank line.
The bottom line. The line where my students felt the most hopeless. The most
powerless.

    After reading *The Hate U Give* (*THUG*) with my students, I created a poetry
contest to give them a chance to attend a private screening of *THUG* on opening day. I asked seven people in my life to judge the contest. All of the judges had
read the book and were ready to be of service. We all thought the judging process
would be a lot easier than it turned out to be. There were forty-five entries. The
judges went six rounds, narrowing down their top four choices (and three honorable mentions), but we could have only four winners because the prize consisted
of my paying their way in and buying their concessions—so yeah; funds were
limited. I called in two more judges and asked them to read all of the judges'
choices and decide on the four winners. After the winners and honorable mentions
were finally identified, one of the judges met us at the movie theater and paid for
EVERYONE's tickets! What?!? After the contest and the private screening and
lunch downtown, we went to Starkville Community Theater, where students were
introduced to several of the judges and to the creators of *The Streetcar*, Mississippi
State University's creative arts journal. Then students took the stage to perform

their poems about *THUG*. After many performances, a panel of student volunteers took the stage and led their peers in a discussion about *THUG*, both the novel and the movie. It was incredible to see my students taking charge of the discussion and expressing their views on such powerful topics as police brutality, code switching, and gang violence.

Write That I . . .

Write that I provided for my family.
Write that I was the one to wipe my little brother's tears, because my mom wasn't around.
Write that I'm doing everything on my own, even though I'm a kid still.
Write that I was caring, that I wasn't a bad person.
Write that I was right there whenever my grandmother called.

Don't write that I was a thug, or that it was drugs that I slung.
Don't write that I hustled so that our lights wouldn't get turnt off.
Don't write that I lived in Garden Heights.
Don't even write that my skin color is 4 shades darker than those who are white.

Write that I didn't do anything to be pulled over.
Write that I never disrespected that cop.
Write that I was harassed right in front of you.

Don't write that I was tough, or strong, or that I put up a fight for my last breath.
Don't write that I suffered.
Don't write of what my last words were.

Write that I mattered.
Write that injustice is unfair.
Write that Officer 115 murdered me because of his assumptions.
Write that I am Khalil, and that I am a long living legacy.

—*Chloe Hickman, Grade 9*

And We Keep Going . . .

We shifted gears in the third nine weeks to look back in time to World War II, to Elie Wiesel's memoir, *Night*. We read chapter by chapter. We discussed chapter by chapter. My students asked the big questions: "How is this possible?" "Why didn't anyone stop this from happening?"

My students wrote poetry to honor the memory of Elie Wiesel and to try to wrap their minds around the impossible—and they made connections to other

points in history and to today. They did this with poetry; many students fell back
to familiar formats to write about Elie Wiesel, using the "Where I'm From" or the
"Write That I . . ." method to express how Wiesel's memoir made them feel. Others created free verse to honor the memories of those lost in the Holocaust.

The Memories

I should have listened . . .

I should have listened to him,
things might have ended up different that day.
I'm sorry Moishe . . . I'm sorry.

The laws, the Germans.
I wanted to kill all of them,
too many times.

The children,
the horrifying memory of burning flesh.
The memory of riding on a cattle car and seeing someone kill his own father
for a piece of bread.

My father getting hit,
shocked me when i saw it with my own eyes,
for the first time.
But eventually I got used to it.

The hunger for food,
made me feel like I didn't matter
no one mattered.

The death march,
I nearly gave up.
But, the desperation to live kept me going,
not god but myself.

Or so I thought.
But, God carried me on,
he is the one who truly helped me.

My father's sickness,
the struggle to help him.
I tried my best but in the end he died

. . .
and i didn't care
. . .
I didn't care.
And then came freedom,
which didn't faze me.
The look in my eyes when I left,
has never left me.

—*Brayam Munoz*

Why Poetry?

Since the day Helen Mullen put *Cotton Candy on a Rainy Day* in my hands,

I realize I have always
thought in poetry,
short, meaningful lines,
connected and disconnected in time.
I dream in poetry,
wistful moments here and there.
I eat in poetry,
tiny nibbles and big, greedy bites.
I protest in poetry,
harsh, angry words and soft-spoken loving words . . .
I teach in poetry,
the you,
the me,
and the we . . .
In Poetry.

A poet once wrote that the revolution will be televised; I believe the revolution will be a poetry slam led by my students. Why? Because the straightest line between any set of "us" and "them" is the written word. My students write themselves into the world by writing the words that connect us to them. Every day I stand at the door of my classroom and I greet every student. I ask, "How are you today?" and I get "Good." Or "Meh." Or a shoulder shrug. But when I give my students Sacred Writing Time and I ask the same question, I get the honest and for real-answer. Usually, unbeknownst to them, in poetry.

Learning Tracker

As you read Tracei's chapter, did you consider what literature you share with students as mentor texts for writing? Tracei shares "the straightest line from any set of 'us' to 'them' is the written word." How does the act of writing build community in her classroom? In yours? What opportunities do you provide for students to share their writing with their peers? How might you amplify your students' voices so that others can learn from their thinking? How can we move the world through our work within our classroom communities? What is one takeaway you could implement within your teaching soon?

References

Christensen, L. (2000). *Reading, writing, and rising up: Teaching about social justice and the power of the written word.* Milwaukee, WI: Rethinking Schools.

Killgallon, D., & Killgallon, J. (2006). *Grammar for middle school: A sentence-composing approach.* Portsmouth, NH: Heinemann.

National Council of Teachers of English. (2016). *Professional knowledge for the teaching of writing.* Urbana, IL: Author. Retrieved from http://www2.ncte.org/statement/teaching-writing/

The Game Design and Writing Project: Designing a Better World with Project-Based Learning

Chapter Four

Margaret A. Robbins
The Mount Vernon School, Atlanta GA

*I*magine a room full of laughter, growing seventh-grade students playing grammar and figurative language board games and video games with smaller but eager fifth-grade students from the other side of our spread-out independent school campus. The desks are together in groups, sprinkled with painted cardboard game boards, playing cards and game pieces made by hand, and computer screens with innovative music and visual effects. The volume level is higher than usual, but teachers for both age groups are excited about the combined class because the students are engaged with the games and learning new literacy skills. It's like a Game Night party, only in a classroom and without the food and drinks and with education-based games about grammatical and literary concepts.

At the beginning of *Jumanji: Welcome to the Jungle* (Kasdan, 2017), the reboot of the original *Jumanji* (Johnston, 1995) classic film, the new main protagonist gets a copy of the *Jumanji* game, thinking it's a board game, and says that no one "plays board games anymore." The new *Jumanji* is a video game, and it proves to be equally as compelling and equally as dangerous as the board game of the original movie. The newest game literally takes players to another world in which they have to fight for survival. It might be that in our "real world," video games have overtaken board games. But some of my middle school students in Atlanta, Georgia, might beg to differ.

During the fall of the 2017–2018 school year, my seventh-grade students and I embarked on my first ever project-based learning (PBL) adventure, the Game Design and Writing Project. Their task was to design a grammar or literary terms game based on the concepts we had learned and reviewed during the semester. To decide what kind of game to create, my students engaged in two preliminary steps: they interviewed the fifth graders about their game interests, and they watched scenes from the original 1995 *Jumanji* of my own childhood. As a result of these thought-producing launch lessons, approximately 70 percent of my students created board or card games individually or in groups, and approximately 30 percent created video games using Scratch and other electronic scaffolding devices. Those who wanted to create video games were given a list of suggested video game generators and could choose the one that worked best for them. Many students gravitated toward Scratch due to its user-friendly nature and their prior experiences with this platform.

While games served as the vehicle, the work centered on learning grammar and figurative language concepts as well as writing techniques and product-design skills. Throughout the process, students reviewed these concepts and learned both real-world application for narrative and expository writing skills and how writing can contribute to the creation of multimodal products and literacies. Eventually, happy squeals sounded from grades 3, 5, and 6 classrooms alike across five different class periods as my seventh graders played grammar and literary term games with their younger peers, games they themselves had created from various maker cart items, cardboard, small whiteboards, and online video game programs.

Metamediating and Project–Based Learning

Hannah Gerber (2015) argues that gaming involves the process of *metamediating*, rather than getting distracted through multitasking. Metamediating "is the practice of interweaving multiple communicative acts simultaneously (reading, writing, listening, speaking, viewing, and representing) while also engaging in intertextual meaning-making" (p. 99). This idea lends merit to the argument that literacy educators need to expand their in-school curricula to include literacies beyond traditional texts, since, with the rise of technology, many future jobs will require the process of metamediating.

As the concept of New Literacies has evolved, we need to reexamine what communication means in contemporary society and how these changing modes of communication affect literacy instruction (Lankshear & Knobel, 2011; Street, 1998). Likewise, literacy educators need to rethink what we define as writing assignments and to think outside the box about what tasks our students complete. Multimodal texts "incorporate a variety of modes, including visual images, hypertexts, and graphic design elements along with written texts" (Serafini, 2011, p. 342). With the rise of the internet and evolving technologies, students need to be exposed to multimodal reading texts and writing assignments to be prepared for twenty-first-century expectations.

In her 2008 NCTE Presidential Address, Kathleen Blake Yancey described in detail this gradual shift in interactions with written texts, noting that with the development of the World Wide Web, writing has become increasingly more public and social, in addition to more accessible, to a larger audience. Multimodal platforms such as Facebook and blogs now convey information in written texts, pictures, and other modes. Composing a text, therefore, can now move beyond words:

> Historically . . . we compose on all the available materials. Whether those materials are rocks or computer screens, composing is a material as well as a social practice; composing is situated within and informed by specific kinds of materials as well as by its location in the community. (Yancey, 2009, p. 334)

Reflecting Yancey's statements, students participating in the Game Design and Writing Project were involved in the traditional writing process of creating steps to playing the game, composing expository explanations, narrating stories to accompany the games, and creating multimodal products with shapes and colors that conveyed specific messages. I would argue that by evolving definitions of literacy, the games themselves were texts that involved a composing process of critical thinking skills and synthesizing knowledge.

Allowing my students to play out the video games they created in groups with the younger students they interviewed encouraged play in the classroom. Play "is important to learning because it allows groups and individuals the opportunity to learn in environments that are relatively free from risk of failure" (Gerber, 2015, p. 97). One of the norms at my school is "fail up," which is conducive to PBL assignments that allow students to experiment and to fail in their experimentation as part of the learning process. The chance to interact with students in the play process with this particular PBL not only raised the stakes in terms of having an authentic audience, but also allowed for play and informal interaction among school-age peers, who were the target audience of the game. My students were also able to bond over such shared interests as games, the desire to better understand grammar, and fantasy world building.

I wanted my students' game design and writing projects to follow the component parts of project-based learning design principles. When teachers create a PBL assignment, for example, they often consider the following: attending to both standards-based learning and student goals; starting with questions; creating conditions for sustained inquiry (e.g., authenticity, student voice and choice, reflection and critique); and encouraging a public product designed for an authentic audience. Of course, getting feedback from a real audience can be difficult to plan due to the scheduling constraints that all teachers experience. Fortunately, for this project there were enough grammar/composition and all-subject teachers at my school willing to support my project for each of my five classes to have a target audience for the games my students created. Three of my classes partnered with third-grade students, one class with fifth-grade students, and one class with sixth graders.

When discussing PBL possibilities, I would be remiss in not acknowledging that my school has more resources than many. We are a "one-to-one" independent school in which each student has a computer. We have two dedicated makerspaces in our school, larger rooms with supplies such as wood, hardware tools, and paint for building PBL prototypes. We also have shared maker carts in classrooms, smaller versions of these larger makerspaces that fit into a more limited classroom space. I believe there is a strong connection between makerspaces and writers workshop, and I am fortunate to work in an environment where I can bring elements of both into my English language arts classroom.

I used to teach at a middle school where the resources were much more limited. If I had taken on this project at my former school, I think I could still have done it, but I would have had to make modifications. For instance, I probably wouldn't have been able to give the students the option of creating a video game instead of a board game, and students might have had to write out their directions and explanatory paragraphs rather than typing them, due to limited access to computers both at the school and in households. It's possible that the games would have been less ornate given fewer resources, yet, importantly, the learning standards could still have been infused in the project.

In addition to this multimodal writing assignment, later in the semester my students wrote fanfiction stories as paratexts, some of which were about games, others of which were about the *Ms. Marvel* comic we read or other fandoms of interest. Paratexts "are those texts, either commercial or fan created, that surround and support the main texts" (Gerber, 2015, p. 100). Increasingly, creating paratexts for classroom settings provides opportunities to improve literacy skills. In my case, when students created narrative stories about being trapped inside their games, they were, in a sense, creating paratexts that supported their game designs. Additionally, they were learning problem-solving skills, as the characters eventually had to find their way outside of the game world.

This fanfiction assignment involved taking an already-created world with characters and creating a new story plot, an assignment that scaffolded the writing process by asking students to balance remaining true to the original stories and creating their own narratives. The Game Design and Writing Project narrative had a similar idea but in some ways was more difficult because the students had to create the character, the world, and the plot, all of which supported the game of their own creation. A few students used characters in their game from favorite movies or television shows, one example being Shrek and Donkey from the popular Disney film—almost a blend between the two assignments. As I look ahead, one curricular change I plan to make is to have my students write fanfiction earlier in the semester, before the Game Design and Writing Project, so the fanfiction story writing process could serve as a scaffold to creating a narrative story centered on a game. I'm hoping the narrative component of the game design project will come more easily to the students as a result, since several students said last year that the narrative was actually the most difficult part of the assignment. One benefit to writing about my practice is that I gain additional insight and reflection and can make adjustments accordingly.

NCTE Position Statement

The NCTE *Professional Knowledge for the Teaching of Writing* position statement offers two critical perspectives on my use of gaming and project-based learning to support writing.

"Composing occurs in different modalities and technologies."

As more specifically related to multimodality, the statement notes that "like all texts, print texts are multimodal: print, whether hand-created or machine-produced, relies for meaning on multiple modalities, including language, layout, and the visual characteristics of the script" (p. xii). Language is represented in many different forms, and particularly in a postmodern society heavy on visual representation, students need to learn how to analyze and produce both traditional texts and texts of alternative form. Games are themselves multimodal texts, as they involve written and verbally communicated rules, game board pieces that represent characters, text written on the board itself, and the movement and manipulation of objects that convey meaning. Thus, my project asked students not only to write in a variety of genres, but also to engage with a variety of texts.

Related to this position statement, I want my students to grapple with postmodern, poststructural definitions of text: "We can think of a text literally in the form of transcripts and books, but to limit the 'text' to those spoken or written words is to limit our understanding of what *counts* as data" (Jackson & Mazzei, 2012, p. 19). Our interactions with one another are texts, and our discourses include the clothes we wear, the objects we manipulate, and the visual elements with which we interact in daily life. Game design thus troubles the definition of traditional texts because it involves texts that go beyond spoken and written words while still engaging these forms of communication.

Multimodality is also related to the idea of social semiotics, which notes that "everything in a culture can be seen as a form of communication, organized in ways akin to verbal language, to be understood in terms of a common set of fundamental rules or principles" (Hodge & Kress, 1988, p. 1). Since game play is a part of American culture, game design also gives students the opportunity to engage in the relationship between culture and communication, which, in my opinion, leads to the development of communities.

"Assessment of writing involves complex, informed, human judgment."

The Game Design and Writing Project asked students not only to build a game using design thinking principles, but also to build a complex game world, instructions for how to play the game, and specific learning outcomes related to grammar and/or literacy skills. There were a lot of moving parts to the assignment that involved a variety of narrative and expository writing skills, in addition to critical thinking skills. The students had to use their judgment as to how game players, particularly those who are their age and younger, would respond to the instructions, and how well they could play the game based on the designed rules and steps.

Additionally, composing a narrative in which they inserted themselves in the game in some way required them to go the extra mile in terms of creative thinking and critical thinking skills. Multimodal writing assignments such as this one ask students to employ skills that involve human interaction, human judgment, and a new understanding of writing composition. Given the game's PBL nature, my students were assessed not only through my teacher-drafted rubric (see Appendix A), but also by their classmates and younger peers who tested out their games and gave them more instantaneous and interpersonal feedback on what worked well and what they might need to tweak for the game to be even more effective. As methods of assessment become more complex with evolving forms of writing, educators should continue to consider how we best help our students receive quality feedback.

The Steps of the Process

The task of the Game Design and Writing Project, based on design thinking and project-based learning principles, was as follows: The students were asked to create a board game or a video game from scratch, writing one to two expository paragraphs explaining the game and the rationale for playing it, step-by-step instructions for how to play the game, and a short one- to three-page narrative story about a player being trapped inside the game and what they experience. The assignment was in the spirit of the original 1995 *Jumanji* film and also took into account changing modes of communication and play, as highlighted in the 2017 version, *Jumanji: Welcome to the Jungle*. For many students, the narrative writing component was the most difficult part of the assignment, but also the most enjoyable. The critical thinking activity of designing a story that encompassed both a narrative arc and the world building of the game encouraged students to look at storying in a different way.

To fully engage in design thinking, my school advocates that our PBL assignments and units involve the following steps: Discover, Define, Design, and Deploy, with empathy as the guiding principle. The Discover step involves a spark or an opening activity, which for me was having the students watch clips of the 1995 *Jumanji* film with Robin Williams and the preview of the then-forthcoming *Jumanji: Welcome to the Jungle* (2017). These viewings sparked an interesting class discussion on how games have changed over time and why games are still relevant in modern society even though they have evolved and changed with the rise of technology.

During the Define stage, students discovered what was tangible and relevant to their upcoming design and took steps toward demonstrating their learning. In this phase of the project, my students interviewed peers from the younger classes about what they like to see in games, what grammatical concepts and/or literary terms they know or want to know, and what they look for in educational games, specifically. They prepared their interview questions ahead of time to help the session go more smoothly. In spite of this advance preparation, some students had an easier time than others getting the information they needed from their younger peers. It was, however, an experience in social interaction and market research.

In the Design phase of the project, students created their prototypes: the board games, computer games, or card games. While a couple of students elected to work independently, most worked in groups of two to four to design their games. They had to learn how to communicate with one another, even through disagreements, and to work with the limited supplies we had in our makerspaces and maker carts. Two students even took the initiative to meet with a faculty member who helped run the larger makerspace on our side of campus in order to obtain additional supplies they needed to create optimal versions of their games.

Having an authentic audience who gives feedback raises the stakes for PBL activities. During the Discover, Define, or Design phases of the project, I would have loved to have experts talk to my students about game design and then give them feedback on the projects at the end. Unfortunately, I was not able to arrange this during the school year due to a tight time schedule and some unexpected constraints, but it is a goal for future years with this project. Still, the target audience aspect helped the projects become more focused.

In the follow-up Deploy session of the project, the students got together to play the games, and the young market researchers saw how their interviewees responded to the games they had created. Since feedback is an important aspect of PBL work, I first had students pair up with another design group in their own class to play each other's games and to give each other suggestions. This activity gave the students time to tweak their games designs before playing them with the younger students. Having their classmates play their games helped some groups realize they needed to revise their step-by-step instructions to make their games more user-friendly for their target audiences. Audience awareness is an important aspect of the writing process in general, whether the audience is small or large, and is indicative of the social aspect of contemporary writing.

When the games, instructions, and explanatory paragraphs were complete at the end of the project (see Appendix B), the students went back to play the games with the same classes they had interviewed. For the most part, the younger student audiences were engaged with the games, although appropriately targeting grammatical concepts for third graders proved more challenging than anticipated for some of my seventh-grade students. Yet the younger students seemed to enjoy playing the games, and my students learned the concepts better through having to create educational games to teach them. Because of the timing of the follow-up activity, the interviewees got to see the results of their input and to have fun while doing so. These student interactions gave middle school students the real-world experience of market research, creating a product, and testing out a product to see how their design worked with actual users.

My seventh graders had to review the grammar and figurative language concepts more thoroughly to create the games based on them, and while playing the games with the younger students, they also taught and reinforced some of the concepts. Seeing how the students responded to the games, particularly the third graders, taught them how to make the content and products age appropriate. My students also had to recognize the difference between learning a concept superficially, learning it well enough to practice the concept, and learning it on a deeper level in order to teach it. Thus, the game creation and play phases of the project proved to be metacognitive. The younger students also benefited from having the grammar and narrative-related literacy terms taught and reinforced.

I feel that I have learned grammar exponentially better by having to teach it, so I wasn't surprised that the same was true for my students. Teaching and interacting with younger students gave the Game Design and Writing Project a real-world, authentic angle that is imperative in a PBL assignment. Although I suspect it would be difficult to teach for an entire semester solely through the PBL approach, I do believe that having students complete one or two PBL units per semester encourages real-world application, along with improving academic and standards-based knowledge.

Following are the more specific requirements for the project assignments and calendar, based on a ninety-minute block schedule:

Task One: Expository (Group)

The first part of your task, with a design team of two to three people, is to create a game that will help students learn a concept related to literacy: reading, vocabulary, writing, and/or age-appropriate grammar concepts (adjective, adverb, verb, etc.). This should be either a board game that people can play in class or a video game that can easily be shared with your classmates and with me via Gmail or Google Docs. Remember that all games have a story line to them, so one skill we can learn is storytelling.

In addition to creating the game itself, you will need to create specific, step-by-step instructions for how we can play it. Assume that we know nothing about your game. Also, write a two-paragraph explanation of your game that would fit on the back of a game box telling us what the game is, what world(s) it involves, why it is fun, and why we should play it. So you are explaining the game to us, but you're also persuading us to buy it from you. ☺

Task Two: Narrative (Individual)

Individually, your task is to write a narrative to accompany your game. You can write either an imaginary story of someone who is experiencing your game (e.g., Mario or Luigi trying to save the princess) or the story of a person who plays the game and benefits from it. The narrative story should be three to five pages long. In addition to a traditional creative essay, you can choose to represent your narrative in comic or graphic form. If you are interested in another multimodal representation of your narrative, please speak with me first.

Schedule of Events (for a block schedule/90-minute class)

Thursday, September 21 (Blue)/Friday, September 22 (Gold):
Watch *Jumanji* previews and begin initial brainstorming of video game, board game, or card game to make.

Monday, September 25 (Blue)/Tuesday, September 26 (Gold):
Prepare interview questions for students ages 3–6. The seventh-grade students will serve the role of Market Researchers, who survey potential subjects' interests in order to more effectively create a product

Wednesday, September 27 (Blue)/Thursday, September 28 (Gold):
Conduct interviews with lower school and younger middle school students to get a better understanding of their interests and knowledge base of literacy skills.

Friday, September 29 (Blue)/Monday, October 2 (Gold):
Students will complete a mini-lesson on writing instructions and on paragraphing. Then they will work in class on game creation.

Tuesday, October 3rd (Blue)/Wednesday, October 4 (Gold):
The students will have a mini-lesson on short fiction pieces: fanfiction, flash fiction, and prose poem narratives specifically. They will then work on their game creations, with the option to play professional games as mentor text models.

Thursday, October 5 (Blue)/Tuesday, October 10 (Gold):
Students will have an opportunity to play professional games to see models and also to "test out" the early versions of their own games and instructions. After doing so, they will adjust their own projects as necessary and test them out with classmates.

Wednesday, October 11 (Blue)/Thursday, October 12 (Gold): Students will have class time to polish their games and write their narrative accounts.

Friday, October 13 (Blue)/Monday, October 16 (Gold): Possible Skype sessions with gaming/comics writing experts. Students will have time to finish their narrative stories and also to finish their game products/expository writing.

Tuesday, October 17 (Blue)/Wednesday, October 18 (Gold): Time to catch up on projects as needed.

Thursday, October 19 (Gold)/Friday, October 20 (Blue): Final deadline and an opportunity to share their work with the younger students so the students can play their games and hear their writing accounts.

Designing a Better World

A major guiding philosophy of my school is "design a better world." My students took small but meaningful steps in this direction by designing games that would help students their age and younger better learn grammatical concepts and literary terms. They also learned how to create products that will engage twenty-first-century learners and that utilize effective storytelling techniques.

Based on feedback I received from the students in semester evaluations, self-reflections, and surveys specifically related to the project, I believe they learned skills related to collaboration and how to best work as teams to create and market a product. They also had to figure out how both narrative and expository writing contributed to the effort, and they learned related writing skills while reinforcing grammar skills and literary terms that their games taught the younger students. Writing can often be a solitary process. Although most students did the narrative component of the assignment individually, the vast majority collaborated with their classmates on the instructions and explanatory paragraphs and learned that writing can be a social process when appropriate.

One student's first semester final exam written reflection was indicative of other important lessons my students learned related to the creative process: "I discovered that the creative process is more complicated than I thought. I learned that I had to be open to all ideas. I also found out that sometimes, your instinct is right the first time. . . . I also found it helpful to take a break when I was stumped." Over time this student found a way to merge her love for Halloween, mythology, plays, and language all into one grammar game, in which the Grinch saves Halloween. The idea came to her while watching the October 2017 middle school performance of *Seussical Jr.*, during which she was giving herself a break from working on the project. While she was watching the play, she realized she needed to trust her initial instinct to have a Halloween theme, since her young testers were going to be playing the game in October. She decided to add the character of the Grinch, but as a savior figure rather than a thief. An important aspect of the creative process that my student learned is that, when possible, it's best to take a break from the project to let one's ideas marinate.

I too learned about the creative process, only from a teacher's perspective. I learned more about how to achieve balance between structure and freedom for the students; specifically, I'm glad that I gave my students voice and choice in this project, but in the future, I want to provide more guidance about where they should be in the game design and writing process at various points in the project. Some students ended up doing a lot of work late in the process, which was due in part to their emerging executive functioning and time management skills as young adolescents. However, now that I have taught this project once, I will better know how to guide time management for my future students.

In a blog I keep as a literacy educator who reflects on her readings and practice, I elaborated on what I learned from implementing my first fully developed PBL unit. I learned to be open to different approaches, as some of my students were much more knowledgeable about video game design and coding than I had realized, thus exposing me to some user-friendly programs that are available for students and online techniques for game design. I learned that collaborating with other classes is a time-consuming process due to logistics, but it's worthwhile because my students and the partnering classes got the real-world opportunity to work with new people. I was proud of how my students conducted themselves with the younger kids, and they seemed to view the interview and game-playing activities as opportunities for leadership in addition to teaching.

I learned to be flexible in my planning and to aim high with expectations, as students have a way of rising to meet high expectations. As mentioned earlier, the part of the assignment that involved putting themselves/characters inside of a game and writing a story was a challenge for some, but it was also a good critical thinking exercise that generated imaginative stories. I was glad I gave the students the option to have their character either within the game or playing the game, because it gave them a chance to innovate some of the world-building qualities of their games.

Toward the end of the school year, I came to realize that a key lesson I had taught my students through the game design project was how to form an *affinity space* (Gee, 2004, 2005). Building on the ideas of Lave and Wenger's (1991) communities of practice, the affinity space "can serve as a 'place' where . . . knowledge is dispersed among the participants and the tools provided within the space, and in which participants use it as a 'strong generator' to develop new, creative products and projects" (Hayes & Duncan, 2012, p. 8). Given the age of my students, I believe this group work helped them to develop their critical thinking skills as well as their Mount Vernon Mindsets, a set of principles and norms that guide our decision making as a school (innovator, solution seeker, communicator, creative thinker, collaborator, and ethical decision maker), particularly the communicator and collaborator roles. When students develop these skills, they are better able to engage in civil discourse and participate as leaders in their various communities, both the ones they create and the ones in which they choose to participate.

The common learning objectives for this project were for the students to develop a better understanding of grammatical and literary terms. The common interests revolved around game playing, both digital and board. Over time, students in my classes, first semester Comics Club, and second semester Creative Writing/Fanfiction Club would learn how to center activities on shared interests, regardless of skill level. These shared interests are part of what connected my students to their younger peers, and part of why students gathered in my clubs to talk about comics and the writing they had created.

At the end of the school year, a small group of my seventh graders decided they wanted to take their learned interests in games, comics, fanfiction, and other elements of popular culture to another level by engaging in out-of-school activities related to these passions. They had become increasingly passionate and interested in "geek culture" as the school year progressed as a result of their engagement with these in-class affinity spaces. Per the students' request, I created a list of comics, young adult literature, and bookstore, comic shop, game shop, and popular culture convention recommendations, some of which they could engage with over the summer as enrichment. The focus on building multimodal literacy skills was exciting to their parents, and the students were happy to engage with one another socially over shared interests and passions. During the 2018–2019 school year, we continued to meet most Friday mornings as a Fandom Club, and we discussed previews of upcoming pop culture films of interest as well as novels.

Perhaps this common passion, more than the learning of grammar and literacy skills, is what bonded students across classes in this project. I believe that people have a deep-seated desire for community building, and an important aspect of community building is becoming a good communicator. If schools were to teach more multimodal literacy skills as a way to build community through communication, perhaps the resulting affinity spaces could create more common bonds between students in our current sociopolitical environment, in which many people feel polarized. Possibly, in the spirit of writing for a better world, such creative collaborative projects can help students see that we are more alike than we are different in our desire to communicate and build community.

Learning Tracker

As you read Margaret's chapter, did you consider how you have approached previous collaborative projects in your classroom? What opportunities do you provide for students to gamify their learning? In what ways can problem solving and critical thinking strengthen writing? What various genres and modes of writing do you encourage in your classroom? What opportunities do you provide for students to grapple with complicated issues that are poised to impact a larger community? What is one takeaway you could implement within your teaching soon?

Appendix A: Rubric for Game Design Project

Component I: Game Design **Number of Points: 35** **Total: ___/35**	Collaborates with group members and does his/her fair share. Game shows evidence of knowledge of the literacy concept. Game shows innovation, creative thinking, problem solving, and solution seeking. Succeeds in teaching a concept related to literacy (grammar, writing, figurative language, etc.).
Component II: Directions and Paragraphs Explaining the Game **Number of Points: 30** **Total: ___/30**	The directions are clear, concise, and easy to follow; people can play the game without the makers explaining it verbally. The paragraphs clarify the rationale of the game and how to play it. They also convince people of the game's relevance and importance. Free of grammar and punctuation mistakes. Paragraphs are structured effectively.
Component III: Narrative (2–5 pages, not to exceed 5 pages) **Number of Points: 35** **Total: ___/35**	Shows evidence of a relationship to the game. Is in fantasy, fanfiction, comic, or narrative/game form. Is free of grammar and punctuation mistakes and stylistically well written. Shows innovation, creative thinking, and solution seeking.

Total: ___/100

Appendix B: Visual Examples of Games

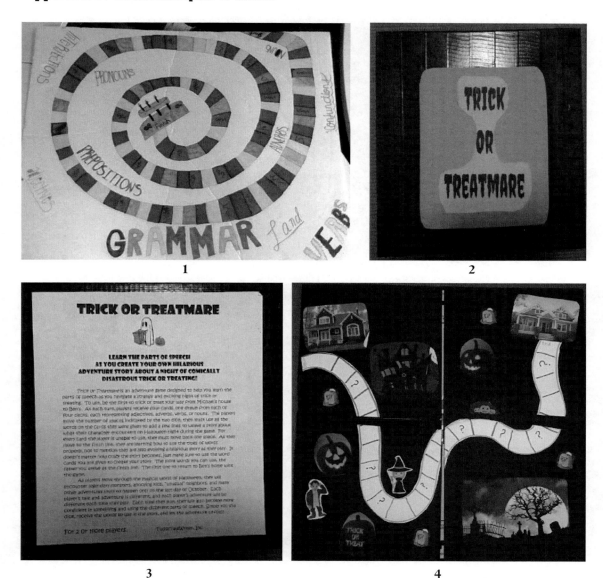

Image 1: The students created the board game Grammar Land using Candy Land as a mentor text. The game gave younger students a chance to learn about parts of speech.

Image 2: The game board box for Trick or Treatmare, the game in which the Grinch saves Halloween.

Image 3: These are paragraphs describing Trick or Treatmare and convincing people to buy and play the game.

Image 4: This is the game board design for Trick or Treatmare.

References

Gee, J. P. (2004). *Situated language and learning: A critique of traditional schooling.* New York, NY: Routledge.

Gee, J. P. (2005). Semiotic social spaces and affinity spaces: From *The Age of Mythology* to today's schools. In D. Barton & K. Tusting (Eds.), *Beyond communities of practice* (pp. 214–32). New York, NY: Cambridge University Press.

Gerber, H. (2015). Hacker heuristics and intertextuality in video games and English language arts. In S. Eckard (Ed.), *Yin and yang in the English classroom: Teaching with popular culture texts* (94–107). Lanham, MD: Rowman & Littlefield.

Hayes, E. R., & Duncan, S. C. (2012). *Learning in video game affinity spaces.* New York, NY: Peter Lang.

Hodge, R., & Kress, G. (1988). *Social semiotics.* Cambridge, UK: Blackwell Publishers.

Jackson, A. Y., & Mazzei, L. A. (2012). *Talking with theory in qualitative research: Viewing data across multiple perspectives.* New York, NY: Routledge.

Johnston, J. (Director). (1995). *Jumanji* [Motion Picture]. United States: TriStar Pictures.

Kasdan, J. (Director). (2017). *Jumanji: Welcome to the jungle* [Motion Picture]. United States: Sony Pictures.

Lankshear, C., & Knobel, M. (2011). *New literacies: Everyday practices and social learning* (3rd ed.). Maidenhead, UK: Open University Press.

Lave, J., & Wenger, E. (1991). *Situated learning: Legitimate peripheral participation.* New York, NY: Cambridge University Press.

National Council of Teachers of English. (2016). *Professional knowledge for the teaching of writing.* Urbana, IL: Author. Retrieved from http://www2.ncte.org/statement/teaching-writing/

Serafini, F. (2011). Expanding perspectives for comprehending visual images in multimodal texts. *Journal of Adolescent and Adult Literacy, 54*(5), 342–50.

Street, B. (1998). New literacies in theory and practice: What are the implications for language in education? *Linguistics and Education, 10*(1), 1–24.

Yancey, K. B. (2009). 2008 NCTE presidential address: The impulse to compose and the age of composition. *Research in the Teaching of English, 43*(3), 316–38.

Part III
Writing
That Heals
the World

In Part I, we explored ways that middle level teachers are working alongside their students to grow their confidence in writing and encourage them to enter the larger conversations of the world through their words. In Part II, we experienced the power of amplified voices, as both teachers provided opportunities for students to grapple with projects and issues that spoke to them and impacted the world through their creative expression and problem solving. Now in Part III, we share two different approaches to writing that position students to use their writing in more empathetic ways. From the micro perspective, Lauren and Joe collaborate on a shared writing experience with middle school and high school students to convey messages of sympathy. This authentic writing assignment provides students the opportunity to practice empathy and compassion for others while also building their confidence in having difficult conversations. From a macro perspective, Matthew involves his middle school students in decision making through in the creation of public narratives that attend to issues of concern in their own lives and the life of the larger community. These teachers and students use the power of writing to heal the damage caused by loss or through the mistreatment of others or the mismanagement of resources, drawing attention to the responsibility and civic duty we each have to use our words for the better.

Learning Tracker

As you read Part III, Writing That Heals the World, consider the roles that sympathy and empathy play in your classroom community. In what ways do you encourage students to express their thoughts and concerns through writing? When students have a choice in their projects, how does it impact their engagement and motivation? How do the skills students hone in your writing classroom transfer to their lived experiences outside of school?

Conveying Sympathy through Carefully Crafted Words: Rehearsal Meets Reality

Lauren Zucker
Northern Highlands Regional High School, Allendale, NJ

Joseph S. Pizzo
Black River Middle School, Chester, NJ

*T*hree years ago, I (Joe, a middle school ELA teacher) helped to comfort the parents of a young lady who had a fatal stroke in church. A year later, in that same location, I gave comfort to an usher who had just lost his father. On both occasions, when the distress of others was palpable, I chose my words extremely carefully. Recalling the challenging nature of my own experiences, I recognize that showing sympathy to someone experiencing intense grief is challenging. We both (Joe and Lauren) believe that the genre of sympathy writing can become a part of our students' experiences in school.

When expressing sympathy to others, one must attempt to convey sympathy with calmness, sensitivity, and support, rather than stating solutions, such as "you should try to . . ." or "for a similar problem, I . . ." As grief expert O'Connell advises, "No analysis of grief and consolation is helpful if its results are merely superficial consolations" (2009, p. 5).

The fine art of giving comfort is a skill important not only in language arts class, but also in life. Schools are increasingly focusing on the need for social and emotional learning (SEL) instruction. SEL has been defined as "the process of acquiring and effectively applying the knowledge, attitudes, and skills necessary to recognize and manage emotions; developing caring and concern for others; making responsible decisions; establishing positive relationships; and handling challenging situations capably" (Zins & Elias, 2006, p. 1). All of the skills embedded in this definition are at the heart of what we call the "comfort note exercise." Both of us are ELA teachers, and we have adopted the position of SEL researchers who argue that SEL competencies can and should be developed in school (Durlak, Weissberg, Dymnicki, Taylor, & Schellinger, 2011)—a philosophical stance that was strengthened after observing our own students' growing capacities to express sympathy through writing.

Professional Knowledge for the Teaching of Writing

The NCTE *Professional Knowledge for the Teaching of Writing* position statement (2016) offers an important approach into our teaching of writing for the purposes of providing comfort to others. Specifically, we want to highlight two statements that we see as working in conjunction with the other aspects of community building and comfort as a social-emotional skill.

"Writing is embedded in complex social relationships and their appropriate languages."

Writing expressions of sympathy and advice to others brings an additional level of complexity to an already difficult social dynamic. These kinds of writing tasks have a clear target audience in mind, which might seem to make the writing less difficult. Writing to someone who is grieving a loss of any kind requires a particular sensitivity and concern in word choice and tone. And it also requires a certain level of understanding that the message of comfort given may not be received as intended. The complexities of the relationship between written word and verbal expression can also complicate the social dynamic.

"Writing has a complex relationship to talk."

One important aspect of writing for comfort is being able to verbally express the same messages of comfort when necessary. Practicing comfort notes in writing allows students to build confidence in their word choice and reduce the uneasiness that often accompanies consoling those who are hurting or grieving. Allowing students the opportunity to talk through their writing approach with their peers as well as hear themselves express or read aloud their own writing provides a deeper insight into the writing itself.

The Comfort Note: Joe's Classroom

Black River Middle School, a nationally recognized School to Watch, is a public school nestled at the top of a rise in Chester, New Jersey. I have been teaching in Chester for forty-four years, after spending my first year in another district. The demographics of my students have changed over the years, but the climate in the community has remained supportive and caring. Students' ability levels may vary, but my students have always been generous in their willingness to help others in need. This altruistic spirit is supported by a community that recognizes the rewards helping others can provide for those who are "extending their hands" to help.

I realize that certain individuals in the world have a knack for making others feel less stressed, even in the most challenging circumstances. One of the main goals of my lesson is to provide my students with a strategy to help others that is supportive and focused on both the individual needing help and the individual offering the assistance. After planning to read Ernest Hemingway's short story "A Day's Wait" (2001) in class and then witnessing an unexpected tragedy in church, I was inspired to create a lesson that would equip my students with their own strategy to provide comfort in a nontraditional yet effective way.

I designed a "comfort note" assignment to give students a chance to practice offering words of comfort with sensitivity to others' needs, all while developing their attentiveness as writers to word choice and tone. We discussed first "The Elements of Giving Advice Effectively" (see Figure 5.1) as a mentor text for giving suggestions to others in a constructive but kind way.

In "A Day's Wait," because of a misunderstanding, a young boy, Schatz, mistakenly believes he's dying. I invited my students to write comfort notes to ease Schatz's emotional distress. After delicately stating to Schatz that "I heard you may be dealing with a challenge," students muted their "I" voice. Word choice was crucial since the task requires putting Schatz's needs first. In addition to the elements listed above, I added the following instructions to assist students in writing their message:

1. Connect. Say something pleasant before mentioning that Schatz may have an issue. Use positive phrases such as "somewhat unfortunate" or "challenging" instead of "I" phrases. As negotiations expert Voss advises, "the word 'I' . . . says you're more interested in yourself than the other person" (Voss, Raz, & Kramer, 2016).

2. Suggest possible solutions without making specific demands: "Consider this" rather than "You should."

3. Reassure Schatz that he can reach out for help in the future.

This model equipped students with new strategies for giving comfort, and the results were wonderful. My students' notes demonstrated a developed ability to choose their words with kindness and sensitivity to another's needs, all while making text-to-self connections.

My student Anushka (2018) writes to Schatz that he "must feel great relief [after learning that he will live]" and "he has most likely learned an impactful lesson." She delicately suggests that Schatz "consider coming to reliable conclusions by checking trusted sources next time."

> Dear Schatz,
> I hope that you quickly recover from the tragic misunderstanding you had with your fever. If I ever come across a situation similar to the one you are experiencing, I definitely would have overreacted. However, you did a great job using your coping skills.
>
> It seems to me that you have struggled with interpreting information that has not yet proven to be accurate. On the bright side, you must feel great relief and have most likely earned an impactful lesson.
>
> Talking about lessons, learning the metric system might greatly help you if you were ever to encounter a scenario similar to the one you have just had. As a suggestion, you may wish to consider coming to ensured conclusions by checking trusted sources next time.
>
> If at any moment you need assistance or guidance, then feel free to reach out to me. As your friend, I know that you'd do the same for me. I hope you enjoy the rest of your day!
>
> Sincerely,
> Anushka

In her comfort note, Ana Clara (2018) reminds Schatz that "I will always be here for you" and "if I ever need help in the future, then you can help me."

> Dear Schatz,
> How are you? I heard about your recent encounter with influenza; what a horrible experience that must have been. I feel sincerely sorry for you.
>
> It seems that you were extremely worried about the fever you had because you had apparently confused Celsius with Fahrenheit. This is a simple mistake. You see, since you had spent time in France, your brain may have still been wired to fit the standards and customs there. As I had stated before, this is a common mistake and you may not want to worry about this.
>
> Now that you have learned the difference between Celsius and Fahrenheit, I'm sure this won't happen again! If it does, however, then you may wish to think about

Figure 5.1. Joe's suggested elements of effective advice giving.

The Elements of Giving Advice Effectively

- Be a good listener/observer.
- Find the "good" and acknowledge it.
- Avoid making direct statements. Instead, recognize that there *seems* to be some difficulty.
- Be empathetic, but don't talk about yourself and your own problems.
- Make the following offers.
  - Present a possible proactive solution, being sure to "suggest" rather than "dictate."
  - Reassure that you "will be there" in the future if you are needed.
- Conclude with a positive message: "Have a nice day" or "I look forward to chatting with you again."

Black River Middle School students authoring their comfort notes to Schatz in Hemingway's "A Day's Wait." (Photo by Joseph S. Pizzo.)

asking a question or two so you can learn the best way to apply facts accurately. This not only applies to situations similar to your past one but also to all of life as well!

Schatz, just know that I will always be here for you in the future should you need my assistance. Maybe if I ever need your assistance in the future, then you can help me!

I look forward to chatting with you again.

Your friend,
Ana Clara

Claire also encourages Schatz by her offer to be available should he need her and looks forward to hearing from him again.

Dear Schatz,
I enjoy our corresponding and always enjoy receiving your notes.

I am sorry about your fever and how you seemingly mistook your temperature for 102.7 degrees Celsius instead of Fahrenheit. That must have been so scary for you to think that you were going to infect your family, possibly condemning them to the same fate you apparently thought you were facing.

I think you did a very good job handling the situation. I definitely couldn't have coped with that challenge as well as you did. After this event, you may wish to learn both the metric and the customary systems to prevent similar things from happening in the future.

As your friend, I hope you know that I am always here if you need help with anything. I hope that I can come to you if I need anything as well. I hope you are feeling better, and I can't wait to hear from you again.

Sincerely,
Claire

To enhance the assignment, I also added a digital option for students to record their voices on platforms such as Powtoon, Adobe Spark, iMovie, and Screencastify. The digital format highlights the sincerity in their voices and encourages student choice.

I shared my idea with Lauren, a high school English teacher who had been working to implement more social-emotional learning lessons in her own classroom (Zucker & Kiely, 2018), and she was immediately intrigued. I reiterated my standing offer to have our students connect classrooms. Together, Lauren and I thought through some of the anticipated benefits. I could share my students' comfort notes to a fictional character with Lauren's students, who would then reach a wider audience and receive feedback on their own writing from more experienced student authors. For their part, critiquing younger students' work might help Lauren's students see themselves as writing coaches with expertise to offer. Though I had conceived of the exercise as an opportunity to help student writers with word choice and tone, connecting classrooms could also help our students write for a more authentic audience and develop the skills of peer feedback and revision.

The Comfort Note: Lauren's Classroom

"The anonymity of the internet makes people mean."

"Kids these days don't know how to talk to each other without using devices."

"Proper sentence structure has been destroyed by texting language."

During my day job as an English teacher, I regularly hear statements like these about students from my colleagues, from parents, and even from students themselves. As an educator and a researcher, I am interested in the ways that technologies impact our social interactions and perceptions. Whether the above statements are fair or accurate, new technologies have undoubtedly changed the ways we live and learn.

Over my thirteen years teaching English, I too have experienced a technological shift. As an early-career teacher, I recorded grades and lessons in print planning books. I wrote (and rewrote) assignment instructions and due dates on the chalkboard. And if I wanted my students to type their essays, I signed out the computer lab weeks in advance.

Perhaps the most significant cultural shift in school over my teaching career has been the evolution toward today's omnipresence of personal digital devices. Whereas students used to keep their phones in their lockers for fear of confiscation or detention, today students spend the majority of the school day moving between their cell phone and a school-issued computer. Students still cluster together in the hallways and in the cafeteria, but more often than not, their heads are turned toward their screens.

Considering how much time we all spend on devices, I try to be strategic about my use of technology in the classroom. On occasion, I announce a "tech-free Tuesday" or "no-tech Wednesday," and fashion a learning environment independent of the internet. And perhaps in response to growing suspicions that the internet has changed our social skills, I began developing lessons to help students practice face-to-face communication and social-emotional awareness (Zucker, 2018; Zucker & Kiely, 2018). When my friend and colleague Joe Pizzo told me about a tech-free writing prompt that could encourage students to put themselves in someone else's emotional shoes, I was immediately interested.

After Joe shared his enthusiasm and assignment instructions with me, I considered how best to adapt the task for my high school students and sought advice from two school social workers. I revised Joe's instructions with a few language tweaks and additions (see Figure 5.2). For example, I renamed Joe's "The Elements

Figure 5.2. Lauren's adaption of Joe's elements of giving advice.

Offering Sympathy Effectively

1. Be a good listener or observer. Demonstrate that you've paid attention to their problem and noticed their reactions.
2. Sympathize with and validate the other person's feelings (acknowledge the validity of their feelings). But don't tell them the story of your own, similar problems.
3. If you think it might help, find a positive aspect of the character's situation and acknowledge it.
4. Make the following offers:
    ○ Offer concrete ways in which you can help, being sure to suggest rather than dictate.
    ○ Remind them that you will continue to support them in the future.
5. Conclude with a kind message.

Things to Remember

- Everyone handles things very differently. People don't always show their emotions. What might not be a big deal for you, could be a big deal for someone else.
- Tell the person you are there for them.
- Sometimes you just need to listen.
- Don't ask for the painful details. ("If you *want* to talk about it, I'm happy to listen.")
- Don't make it about yourself.

of Giving Advice" to "Offering Sympathy Effectively" because my colleagues and I felt our students needed to practice listening to others instead of rushing to insert their opinions or talk about themselves. I also added a list of tips such as "everyone handles things differently" and "sometimes you just need to listen."

When it was time to deliver the lesson, I began with a discussion about the language we use to offer each other sympathy. Students gave several suggestions (e.g., "I'm here for you."). I asked students to talk about what it feels like when they are looking for comfort but a friend or parent responds insensitively. Students gave several examples of what *not* to say to someone who is hurting (e.g., "Get over it."). After sharing instructions, I provided writing time. Students chose one character from the book they were reading (*The Little Prince* by Saint-Exupéry [2000]) who they thought could use some sympathetic words. To avoid spoiling the book for Joe's students, I asked mine to provide character pseudonyms. Here is ninth grader Olivia's comfort note:

> Dear Avi,
>
> I am so sorry about you and Paul not being able to see each other anymore. Losing a friend can be hard, especially when you have such a close connection with them. Even though you two are far apart, everything will be alright. Knowing that this is hard, I want you to know that I am here for you if you need it. I will support you, encourage you, and be there if you just want to talk. Also, if it would help, I can recreate activities you and Paul did together. I will always be there for you and I hope you keep this in mind. Even though you think you might have lost a friend, don't worry because you have another one right here.
>
> Your Friend,
> Olivia

I was pleased with my students' efforts to express sympathy with sensitivity and care. When I later revealed to students that they would be sharing their notes with seventh graders working on a similar assignment, they were excited by the prospect of working with younger writers.

Real-World Applications in Lauren's Classroom

Just a few weeks later, the world was shaken by the tragic news of a school shooting in Parkland, Florida. To help the school community offer support, a teacher at my school created a banner for students to write messages to the victims and their families. I was struck by the relevance of Joe's activity to this current catastrophe. Accepting an administrator's invitation to bring my class down to sign the banner, I hoped that the skills would transfer. Though they had practiced on a fictional character, now my students attempted to find the words to comfort students their own age who had experienced unexpected trauma and loss. While many struggled to summon the right words, several of my students took the time to write longer, personalized messages to express their sympathy. Others went further, encouraging Parkland students to take action and pledging their support. Though the primary goal of the comfort note activity was simply to practice offering sympathy through interpersonal communication, this practice could serve as a first step toward larger-scale, action-oriented responses to injustice or trauma.

Northern Highlands Regional High School students signing a banner for victims of the school shooting in Parkland, Florida. (Photo by Doreen Albano.)

Connecting Middle and High School Classrooms

Joe shared his students' writing with Lauren after receiving student and parent permission, as well as removing students' last names from their work. Lauren's students read their work eagerly, captivated by the seventh graders' maturity and effort.

Lauren asked students to respond directly on a shared document so that Joe's students could easily access their feedback. Lauren instructed students to give the seventh-grade writers specific compliments, which they provided with ease:

> I liked how you were empathetic with the person who you were writing to without making it seem as though you were talking about yourself. Also, you really reassured

the receiver that their mistake is common. Great job!

I like how you made sure to tell the person that the mistake that they made was completely normal. It would be very reassuring to whoever is receiving the letter.

Since this was Lauren's students' first contact with the seventh graders, she restricted their comments to positive feedback, worried that constructive criticism would be more difficult to manage. In retrospect, she might have encouraged her students to also give tips for improvement. In the future, she plans to modify her instructions to encourage students to provide and receive more authentic feedback (Dawson, 2009; Graff, 2009; Lindblom, 2015; Wiggins, 2009).

Conclusion: Reflecting on the Process

The school year coming to an end, an unfortunate turn of events gave us an authentic "lesson within the lesson." After a lapse in our communication, Lauren reached out to Joe to see if his students had read her students' work. Joe replied that he hadn't had a chance to complete the activity since he had lost both his mother and his aunt within a sixteen-hour period. This time, Lauren found herself in the position of offering sympathy. Penning a reply to Joe's message, she struggled to find the right words. The experience reminded her that we all need ongoing practice treating one another with kindness and empathy. Lauren was also reminded that being a teacher of writing who writes (Anderson & Kraushaar, 2017; Durham, 2017; Rief, 2017) allows her to be vulnerable with her students and better empathize with them as writers.

For Joe, this life lesson has been one of the most vivid and authentic of his career. Not only was he teaching his students an important SEL-based lesson, but to his surprise, he found himself on the receiving end of the lesson he was teaching. Though he had not expected it, the outpouring of kindness and support from his students was overwhelming as they offered their sincere condolences, reassuring him that they would be there to comfort him. This lesson had served its original purpose: everyone had learned how to give comfort by listening, by acknowledging another person's feelings, and by offering ways to support each other through tough situations.

Learning Tracker

In what ways do you engage your students in writing for comfort? How can we use our classroom experiences to build empathy for others? How might you collaborate with other teachers or schools to provide writing feedback to each other? What challenges can authentic writing experiences like this one bring? What might students learn about the power of words to heal the hurts of the world? What is one takeaway you could implement within your teaching soon?

References

Ana Clara. (2018). https://www.powtoon.com/c/cYYiTCNMcCh/1/m

Anderson, P., & Kraushaar, K. (2017). We must write together. *Voices from the Middle, 25*(2), 47–50.

Anushka. (2018). https://www.powtoon.com/c/g8Lp5dIR3CT/1/m

Dawson, C. M. (2009). Beyond checklists and rubrics: Engaging students in authentic conversations about their writing. *English Journal, 98*(5), 66–71.

Durham, S. K. (2017). Some things a poet does: Sharing the process. *Voices from the Middle, 25*(2), 50–54.

Durlak, J. A., Weissberg, R. P., Dymnicki, A. B., Taylor, R. D., & Schellinger, K. B. (2011). The impact of enhancing students' social and emotional learning: A meta-analysis of school-based universal interventions. *Child Development, 82*(1): 405–32.

Graff, N. (2009) Approaching authentic peer review. *English Journal, 98*(5), 81–87.

Hemingway, E. (2001). A day's wait. In A. N. Applebee (Ed.), *The language of literature* (pp. 5–9). Evanston, IL: McDougal Littell.

Lindblom, K. (2015, July 27). School writing vs. authentic writing. *Writers who care*. Retrieved from https://writerswhocare.wordpress.com/2015/07/27/school-writing-vs-authentic-writing/

National Council of Teachers of English. (2016). *Professional knowledge for the teaching of writing*. Urbana, IL: Author. Retrieved from http://www2.ncte.org/statement/teaching-writing/

O'Connell, T. L. (2009). *Dialogue on grief and consolation*. New York, NY: Rodopi.

Rief, L. (2017). Teachers who write (as teachers of writers). *Voices from the Middle, 25*(2), 30–36.

Saint-Exupéry, A. D. (2000). *The little prince*. Boston, MA: Mariner Books.

Voss, C., Raz, T., & Kramer, M. (Narrator). (2016). *Never split the difference: Negotiating as if your life depended on it*. New York, NY: HarperAudio.

Wiggins, G. (2009). Real-world writing: Making purpose and audience matter. *English Journal, 98*(5), 29–37.

Zins, J. E., & Elias, M. J. (2006). Social and emotional learning. In G. G. Bear & K. M. Minke (Eds.), *Children's needs III: Development, prevention, and intervention* (pp. 1–13). Bethesda, MD: National Association of School Psychologists. Retrieved from https://www.wtc.ie/images/pdf/Emotional_Intelligence/eq14.pdf

Zucker, L. (2018). An imaginary party sparks academic conversations. *New Jersey English Journal*, 7, 9–11. Retrieved from https://digitalcommons.montclair.edu/nj-english-journal/vol7/iss1/3/

Zucker, L., & Kiely, J. (2018). Mindful ELA: Lessons from a grassroots wellness initiative. *English Leadership Quarterly*, *40*(4), 10–13.

**Chapter
Six**

"Story of Self, Us, and Now": Writing Public Narratives to Build Community, to Heal, and to Co-Create Curriculum

Matthew Homrich-Knieling
Detroit, MI

*I*t was the third week of school. I slowly paced my classroom with a mix of emotions: admiration, joy, curiosity, and slight anxiousness. My seventh-grade students were scattered about in groups of three to four. They took turns reading aloud their public narratives, telling a personal story about an injustice that affects their lives and about which they are passionate. I remember one group of boys in particular who really leaned into this process, defying the pressures of gender socialization that tells boys and men to numb and hide their emotions. I watched as these four boys demonstrated profound bravery, vulnerability, and trust by sharing their stories; I watched as these four boys demonstrated deep empathy and care by listening intently. I knew that this was an important moment.

English language arts classrooms are a special space, a space where my southwest Detroit students' brilliance, boldness, and bravery can shine. In my seventh-grade ELA classroom, I strive to co-create space for my students to write, read, discuss, and reflect on their experiences, and throughout this process, build curriculum around those lived-experiences.

The majority of my students are Latinx students whose first language is Spanish. There are strong values of community and family within the neighborhood that manifest in my school through familial-like friendships and strong community support networks. However, the city of Detroit has a long history of systemic injustices that created economic insecurity and segregation, issues that persist in the city today. Systemic injustices such as housing insecurity, immigration injustices, racism and discrimination, and gun violence translate to traumas that students might carry, traumas that cannot be ignored or silenced in school. As educators, then, we have an imperative to make our schools and classrooms spaces where our students feel heard and feel as safe as possible. I try to use my classroom as a space for my students to process these experiences when they feel comfortable, to connect personal harm to systemic injustices, to heal from harm, and also to find joy and to celebrate their identities.

Connecting theory to practice, I use this chapter to center the resilience, the profound insights, and the commitment to justice that my students possess. Specifically, I reflect on the transformative possibilities of public narratives, an activist-oriented form of personal storytelling, as a radical, healing, and community-building process.

Reflections on Identity and Pedagogy

During the 2016–2017 academic year, my first year of teaching in southwest Detroit, I made concerted efforts to write curriculum that used reading and writing as tools to interrogate systems of oppression that impact my students, to learn from people and movements who have fought for justice, and to celebrate my students' identities. We read poems such as "For the 'Capitol Nine'" by Francisco X. Alarcón and "In Response to the Man Who Asked, 'Why Do Your People March for Everything?'" by Andrea Hernández Holm and watched videos about topics like Standing Rock protestors and #BlackLivesMatter. Contrary to my intentions, my students oftentimes seemed disengaged and disempowered with this curriculum. The summer following that school year, however, I reflected seriously on my curriculum, read critical education and literacy scholarship, and imagined new pedagogical possibilities, and I started to see the problems in my classroom more clearly. Prior to and throughout my units, I had not critically reflected on my own identity as a white educator teaching in a community of color in which I did not grow up. Because of this, I was pushed to recognize that if I wanted my curriculum to be oriented around justice and healing, I needed to rethink the ways in which I engaged in curriculum design so as to not reproduce oppressive dynamics. Rather than creating curriculum *for* my students, I recognized the transformative potential of creating curriculum *with* my students. In other words, I started to understand how to create a curriculum that offered space for my students to define their own cultural, linguistic, and community identities, and then recursively built out a curriculum that lifted up those identities and experiences.

These understandings led me to ask myself critical and necessary questions about my pedagogy. Namely, I was left wondering: *How can writing be a tool to involve my students in the curriculum design process, to build trust and community, and to heal?*

One way that I started to answer these questions and to create curriculum that offered my students space and agency to contribute to its creation was through writing public narratives, a form of writing commonly used among community organizing groups. My plan was to start the following school year by writing public narratives, and my hope was to use this writing practice as a way for my students to build community, to heal from harm, and to reclaim agency. The topics, texts, and discussions that would make up my subsequent units, then, would explicitly and directly respond to and center the experiences and stories that my students shared.

What Are Public Narratives?

The overall purpose of public narratives is to center one's own personal story within a larger systemic, sociopolitical injustice, to position oneself and one's community as integral players in creating solutions to this systemic problem, and to motivate others to join you in working for justice. A public narrative, then, is "a leadership practice of translating values into action" (Ganz, 2011, p. 274). Public narratives comprise three sections: the story of self, the story of us, and the story of now. The *story of self* focuses on "choice points—moments when we faced a challenge, made a choice, experienced an outcome, and learned a moral" (p. 283). In other words, if your public narrative is grounded in organizing people around unjust discipline in schools, your story of self might share a personal experience of being treated unfairly in school. The second portion, *story of us*, connects the values and experiences rooted in one's story of self to a larger community of people affected by this issue. The final portion, *story of now*, grounds the public narrative in the current context of the struggle; it "articulates an urgent challenge—or threat—to the values that we share that demands action now" (p. 286). In this final portion, the storyteller is trying to motivate their readers by offering the choice to take action.

Professional Knowledge for the Teaching of Writing

The NCTE *Professional Knowledge for the Teaching of Writing* position statement (2016) offers critical perspectives on my use of public narratives. Specifically, I want to highlight two statements that I see as working in conjunction to position the writing of public narratives as a liberatory and healing process.

"Writing is embedded in complex social relationships and their appropriate languages."

This statement explains how "[i]n every writing situation, the writer, the reader, and all relevant others live in a structured social order, where some people's words count more than others" (p. xi). As this statement suggests, some students' languages, especially the languages of many students of color—African American Vernacular English, Spanglish, etc.—"count less" and are often deemed as inappropriate in academic contexts, a form of linguistic racism that many students of color internalize (Baker-Bell, 2013). However, writing can also be used as a tool to combat those oppressive structures.

The statement goes on to explain that "expert writing teachers deliberately teach students to incorporate their heritage and home languages intentionally and strategically in the texts they write" (p. xi). As a reader, I know that the strategic and dynamic blending of heritage and home languages creates powerful and artful texts; however, as a writer who is monolingual and grew up in a white, middle-class community that largely speaks "standard" English, I have little insight into how to produce those texts. The majority of my students, though, speak Spanish and English; as such, I've found that my role as a writing teacher is to create space for my students' linguistic knowledge to flourish. This means I support my students in claiming their voice; this means I don't correct my student who writes "imma" in his public narrative, as he powerfully declares action he wants to take against injustices; this means I trust my students' decision to incorporate Spanish words that they know articulate a concept or an emotion more accurately. I can't teach my students how to incorporate their many languages into their writing as effectively as I can create space for them to feel safe and encouraged to write in ways that communicate genuinely, powerfully, and dynamically. Then I can use their writing as models for how to fluidly and strategically incorporate their languages into their writing.

"Writing is a tool for thinking."

This principle of the statement, on the other hand, has contributed to expanding my thinking about the possibilities of public narratives. While I've already alluded to using public narratives at the beginning of the school year, I've also revisited public narratives as a "tool for thinking."

During the middle of the 2017–2018 school year, my students engaged in a research project on social injustices. Rather than having students select a topic as an isolated process, I had them revisit and rewrite a public narrative. Because public narratives allow writers to ground a systemic injustice in their personal story, my students could use writing to think about an injustice that connects to their present experiences and then use that injustice as the topic of their research.

Writing Public Narratives

Agency and Trust

Choosing to begin my school year with public narratives certainly felt like a risk, as they require tremendous vulnerability, strength, courage, and trust, and my students and I were all new to this classroom space. Moreover, I didn't want my students to feel like they *owe* anyone their story. To that end, I was intentional about encouraging them to write only about that which they felt comfortable writing. By launching right into public narratives, I also wanted to communicate trust in my students' agency and capacity to tell their own story, their own truth.

To encourage students to begin reflecting on their experiences, their stories, and their visions of a more just world, I tailored my do now/warm-up questions to facilitate this process. As I started to explain public narratives to my students, I asked them, for example, to write, discuss, and share responses to questions such as:

1. What are challenges you've faced in life?
2. Who is the most important person in your life? Tell a story about why that person is important to you!
3. If the world were more fair, what would it look like? What things would change?

These questions not only prompted students to consider how to focus their public narrative, but they also communicated an important message: my classroom is a space where we can bring our full selves, where we can share and listen to one another's stories. Schools are not often a space where students can bring in or even acknowledge their lives beyond the classroom walls, and this is especially true for students of color, who are in an institution that oftentimes maintains and reproduces racist structures, and who are taught by teachers who often do not look or sound like them. As one of my students shared in a reflection after writing her public narrative, "It felt really comfortable, but there aren't many occasions where topics that involve things around you are brought up in school."

I then adapted a graphic organizer (Ganz, 2011) to help students think through the three parts of the public narrative. The first part of the graphic organizer asks students to brainstorm specific experiences that have shaped their story of self. Based on those experiences, the students consider a change they want to make in the world so that they, people they care about, and future generations don't have to share similar experiences. Finally, they start to piece everything together through a more cohesive narrative by considering: What is a current challenge you are facing? What is a choice you could make to take action? And what could be the outcome if you and others took that action? This graphic organizer helped my students to conceptualize their public narrative and establish a focus.

I recognized, though, that I couldn't ask my students to engage in the process of writing a public narrative in an unfamiliar space without engaging in it myself. Therefore, while I explained to my students the purpose and process of public narratives, I shared my own process of writing one. Not only was I trying to model the writing process, but I was trying to demonstrate my own level of vulnerability and trust in this community space we were building (see Figure 6.1).

Figure 6.1. My beginnings toward my own public narrative. (Adapted from Ganz [2011] by Serena Zhang and Voop de Vulpillieres [n.d.])

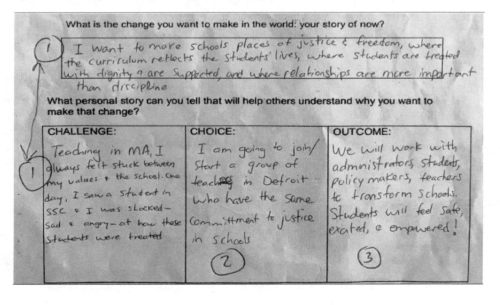

Telling Your Story Freely

My students took a little more than a week to complete their public narratives. Throughout this time, I intentionally didn't provide any direct instruction on writing, grammar, or composition. I wanted my students to own their writing and their voice. I wanted them to tell their stories freely. The majority of my students speak Spanish as a first language, and many have internalized insecurities exacerbated by prescriptive language requirements often found in ELA classrooms. Initially, my students sought answers to questions that would minimize their agency (*Is this word spelled correctly? How long does this have to be? Does this sound okay? How many sentences do we need for each paragraph?*). Most often I responded in ways that shifted the power to my students (*I trust your judgement! However long it needs to be in order to share your story!*), and eventually they developed a deeper sense of confidence and ownership over their writing. Moreover, I took time to intentionally position my students as experts in their storytelling. I have found that student resistance to writing often comes from being told to write about topics that are irrelevant to their lives or that position the teacher as the expert. When I shifted this dynamic by reiterating that each student is the only one who can write that particular public narrative, many of my students developed a confidence that was validating through their writing.

By the end, my students' public narratives were powerful, raw, insightful, and beautiful. They displayed tremendous capacity to write powerfully and boldly. Because I had created space for my students to write in their own voice, I had, for instance, students incorporating Spanish words into their narratives without prompting. These linguistic decisions made without direct instruction allowed their writing to be a truer reflection of their voices and their identities and experiences. This student's introduction to her public narrative demonstrates this profound capacity:

Latino/Americano life

Everybody should feel proud of who they are, no matter gender, race, culture, etc. You should feel comfortable with who they are, and shouldn't change any of that. That's why I'm gonna write about myself and show that hispanic women, men and children, should always have rights to work, learn, and be treated fairly. I'm not just saying this is just for hispanic people, this too is for other races, because we are humans [tambien somos humanos] we should be treated with respect and equally too because you don't know that they had to go through to get this "better" life, full of discrimination and racism, but I don't think people notice that, people just think the world is pink and colorful but in reality {the true world} there's dark colors too {bad stuff} not just pink or whatever, there's bad and good stuff, not just good stuff. But I guess people don't notice that, and we should open their eyes {sus ojos} They are like sharks trying to feed up on tiny fish. When I was little my mom always told me "hija yo quiero que estudies en el U.S. para una vida mejor" that meant "daughter I want you to study in the U.S. for a better life."

Centering Our Stories

After my students finished their public narratives, we took some time to center the experiences everyone was bringing to the classroom. I showed my students a list of all the issues that were addressed in the public narratives and explained how each topic was addressed by more than one student. I wanted us to be aware of what we were all bringing to our classroom space, and more important, I wanted my students to feel a sense of solidarity and community with their peers.

Public Narratives
- Bullying
- Immigration injustices
- Witnessing violence
- Mental health
- Struggles in school (academically/socially)
- Animal abuse
- Environmental problems (pollution, litter)
- Racism/discrimination
- Gender issues
- School meal options
- Physical health issues
- Poverty/homelessness

Following this, my students shared their public narratives in a small group. I allowed them to select their own groups, recognizing that they might not yet be comfortable sharing their story out loud with students they didn't know. Moreover, I encouraged them to only share that which they were comfortable sharing. If that meant skipping or condensing some sections, that was okay. Most important, however, we established some ground rules to ensure that we were creating a space that felt safe for my students to share their stories. After whole-class discussion, we narrowed it down to three ground rules:

1. **Active/Compassionate Listening** (listen attentively and with care).
2. **What is shared in your group stays in your group.**
3. **Share what inspired you and build each other up.**

After we all agreed to adhere to these ground rules, my students split into groups of three to four and took turns reading their stories. As I shared in my opening vignette, it was so beautiful to watch friends listen to each other so earnestly and encourage each other so deeply. Following the process of sharing their public narratives, we transitioned into a unit on injustices and social movements; however, unlike the aforementioned unit from the 2016–2017 academic year, this time I intentionally and explicitly grounded the curriculum of the unit in my students' experiences. I used the personal stories my students shared to create a justice-oriented unit around those stories. Because this subsequent unit was in direct response to my students' stories, there was a more palpable sense of connection and student agency throughout the unit. My students felt more recognized, heard, and participatory.

Conclusion: Themes and Reflections

Throughout this process, my students taught me transformative lessons about the power and possibilities of writing.

Writing as Healing

As my students reflected on the process of writing a public narrative, I learned that the experience offered critical space for healing. Because my students were able to bring their full selves into their writing and into the classroom, they expressed a sense of relief through that experience. As one student reflected, "I felt like I got a lot off my chest. I personally really enjoyed writing about a problem I was facing/faced."

Writing as Community

While the writing portion was largely an independent process, the experience of centering everyone's shared experiences and reading the public narratives in small groups developed in the classroom a sense of community and solidarity. This experience, then, built a foundation of trust from which we could grow as the year progressed. One student, for example, explained how sharing her public narrative out loud "let me tell my story so I feel safe and I trust them." Another student expressed how "everyone's stories inspired me, so I wanted to help them make their change."

Writing as Participatory Culturally Sustaining Pedagogy

One of the theories that underpins a lot of the work in my classroom is culturally sustaining pedagogy (CSP), which builds off the work of Gloria Ladson-Billing's culturally relevant pedagogy (1995). CSP "requires that [our pedagogies] support young people in sustaining the cultural and linguistic competence of their communities" (Paris, 2012, p. 95). Moreover, one of the main goals of CSP is to dismantle the ways in which white supremacy and oppression manifest in schools:

> CSP builds on decades of crucial asset-based pedagogical research that has countered pervasive deficit approaches, working against the backdrop of beliefs in White superiority and the systemic racism they engender, to prove that our practices and ways of being as students and communities of color are legitimate and should be included meaningfully in classroom learning. (Paris, 2016, p. 6)

In the process of writing public narratives, I started to understand the role that writing can play in creating space for students to drive how to meaningfully center their experiences. After the public narratives, my students and I engaged in a unit on stories of resistance and social change. In many ways, they participated in the creation of this unit because the topics and texts we read were in direct response to the stories my students shared in their narratives. This experience demonstrates the critical importance of creating space for students to define their own identities and experiences as part of the process of creating culturally sustaining pedagogy, and, moreover, the transformative role that writing can play in that process.

Learning Tracker

As you read Matthew's chapter, did you consider the ways in which your students are involved in designing the curriculum? What might that look like? Is the curriculum you design relevant to the students you serve? How do you know? What opportunities for public narrative exist within your own communities? How can you use public narratives to impact your school community or communities-at-large? What is one takeaway you could implement within your teaching soon?

References

Baker-Bell, A. (2013). "I never really knew the history behind African American Language": Critical language pedagogy in an advanced placement English language arts class. *Equity and Excellence in Education, 46*(3), 355–70.

Ganz, M. (2011). "Public narrative, collective action, and power." In S. Odugbemi & T. Lee (Eds.), *Accountability through public opinion: From inertia to public action* (pp. 273–89). Washington, DC: The World Bank.

Ladson-Billings, G. (1995). Toward a theory of culturally relevant pedagogy. *American Educational Research Journal, 32*(3), 465–91.

National Council of Teachers of English. (2016). *Professional knowledge for the teaching of writing*. Retrieved from http://www.ncte.org/positions/statements/teaching-writing

Paris, D. (2012). Culturally sustaining pedagogy: A needed change in stance, terminology, and practice. *Educational Researcher, 41*(3), 93–97.

Paris, D. (2016, May). *On educating culturally sustaining teachers*. Retrieved from http://www.teachingworks.org/images/files/TeachingWorks_Paris.pdf

Zhang, S., & de Vulpillieres, V. (n.d.). "Public narrative participant guide." Retrieved from https://www.ndi.org/files/Public%20Narrative%20Participant%20Guide.pdf, https://www.ndi.org/sites/default/files/Public%20Narrative%20Participant%20Guide.pdf

Conclusion: Writing Can Change Everything

Shelbie Witte

It is no longer sufficient to construct curriculum in preparation for later life. It is no longer sufficient for children to learn about decisions adults make for the planet they will inherit. . . . It is their world already.
—Luke et al., 2018, p. 261

In reflecting on my time as a middle school classroom teacher, I'm certain I made the honest mistake of using phrases such as "You will need to be able to do this in the real-world" or "We are preparing you for the real world" without giving much thought to the idea that our students are very much a part of this world already. Much too often, I designed curriculum that was in preparation for a life to come versus the life they were currently living. In contrast, the seven teacher-writers in this collection have opened widely the doors of their classrooms so that we might get a glimpse of how they approach the teaching of writing with their middle level learners and the ways in which they help their students develop a better sense of ownership of their place in this world right now and the communities in which they live.

Each teacher-writer brings with them to this collection a unique set of circumstances that both rewards and challenges them as professionals. It's not unusual for teachers to read chapters in professional books like this one and ponder whether they could achieve the same results with their own students in their own classrooms. While each chapter offers practical approaches as a guide to replicate or inspire the creation of a new unit or lesson appropriate for the reader's individual classroom, comprehensively, this collection of chapters offers a set of pedagogical approaches and themes that are important to consider.

(Re)Considering Your Teaching Approach to Writing

First, there are no prepackaged curricula or formulas featured here. Prepackaged curricula serve a purpose to some extent in very rare circumstances, but we have yet to find one that is effectively responsive to the needs of all of the diverse learners in a particular classroom setting. The teacher-writers featured here are not under a district or school mandate to implement a prepackaged curriculum or a particular approach to writing. That being said, each feels the pressures of showing growth in student reading and writing, as all teachers do. But each has negotiated, in their own way, the autonomy to use their professional expertise in their classrooms to the fullest extent. This is a critical step in breaking away from curricula designed for the masses and moving toward personalized learning tailored to the needs of each student.

Also, there is rarely an instance in this collection where writing is discussed in isolation from reading. We know from decades of research (Daane, 1991; Newkirk, 1982; Stotsky, 1983; Tompkins, 2002) that the likelihood of strong readers becoming strong writers is high. Striving readers and writers learn much about the art and craft of language by reading and writing interchangeably. Therefore, each of these teacher-writers provides a language- and literacy-rich classroom full of books and access to texts in a variety of formats.

As well, you may have noticed a wide range of genres and modes represented in these chapters. Embracing composition in all forms (Yancey, 2009), each classroom recognizes that writing takes on multiple, malleable forms depending on the topic, audience, and purpose. Each teacher-writer guides their students to recognize the importance of knowing how to leverage modality to best meet the writing situation.

Cultivating the Culture of a Daily Writing Community

Each classroom featured in this collection makes space daily for writing. This cultivated space is nonnegotiable, or as Tracei Willis refers to it, sacred. We know that to develop as writers, adolescents need the opportunity to build stamina, experiment with style and voice, and have time to think critically and creatively (Applebee & Langer, 2011; Atwell, 1987; Graham, Gillespee, & McKeown, 2013). As most teachers have experienced, adolescents often struggle with writing on topics outside of their own experiences and interests. Through a daily writing routine, adolescents have a wealth of short writing samples from which to build on in future projects and have opportunities to build their confidence in writing for particular audiences and situations.

In addition to spending time daily on writing, each teacher-writer carves out the necessary time for community building within their classrooms. To do the hard work of writing requires an environment of trust that can only be built over time. Adolescents must learn to trust one another with their own writing as well as be open to the feedback they will receive in peer writing groups. Only when trust is achieved can students begin to feel comfortable sharing difficult things and tackling difficult topics, as modeled by Lauren Zucker and Joseph S. Pizzo. And modeled revision, as shared by Frances Lin, gives students the chance to see writing as an ongoing process, not a final product.

Teacher as Writer

Each chapter in this collection also models the varying roles that teachers fulfill within a classroom writing community. There are many pedagogical implications when teachers are willing to share their own writing with and alongside their students (Calkins, 1993; Graves, 1994; Routman, 1991). A teacher's lived experience as a writer brings greater insight into the challenges their students may also encounter as they grow in their craft. To be vulnerable alongside one's students is not an easy position to take, nor one that comes easily for most. And yet the benefits far outweigh the initial uneasiness, as many literacy leaders (e.g., Linda Rief, Nancie Atwell, Penny Kittle) can attest.

Beyond sharing writing alongside the students in the classroom, it is also important for teachers to share their teaching experiences with a larger audience, much like the teacher-writers in this collection have done. While intimidating at first, perhaps the greatest contribution we can make to the profession is to share openly what our teaching looks like, what's working well, and most important, what's not working and why. To participate in the professional dialogue of our work is to contribute to the growing understanding of the intricacies of education as a whole and the importance of recognizing the expertise of the classroom teacher as the most important factor in student success.

Considering the Bigger Picture of Our Classroom Work

While academic standards serve a purpose, none of the teachers featured in this collection began their approaches or units with the academic standards at the core of the planning. Each started with a larger picture in mind: how can I guide/help my students become the people they want to be? The teacher-writers focused on opportunities for their students to make an impact on their communities or to draw on the critical thinking skills necessary to motivate and initiate ideas. Starting with the larger picture and working inward, it's easy to see how the academic standards fall into place.

These chapters also illustrate the beauty of what happens when students drive the work. As the chapters by Sarah Bonner, Margaret A. Robbins, and Matthew Homrich-Knieling illustrate, when students are allowed to have ownership in projects and choice in topic, they often exceed our expectations in the scope and quality of work. To be an adolescent in 2020 is to be an active member in a participatory culture, and our classrooms should be no different. Learning to compose for a purpose of your own making is perhaps one of the greatest tasks to accomplish, and these middle level learners have modeled for us how well it can be done.

It does not go unnoticed that each of our teacher-writers models a deep commitment to teaching and teaching well, demonstrating a true professionalism and dedication to helping our students discover their "whys," whether it be to share their thinking with the world, to move the world with their ideas, or to heal the world with their actions.

References

Applebee, A. N., & Langer, J. A. (2011). A snapshot of writing instruction in middle and high schools. *English Journal, 100,* 14–27.

Atwell, N. (1987). *In the middle: Reading, writing, and learning with adolescents.* Portsmouth, NH: Heinemann.

Calkins, L. (1993). The lifework of writing. *The Australian Journal of Language and Literacy, 16*(1), 32–37.

Daane, M. C. (1991). Good readers make good writers: A description of four college students. *Journal of Reading, 35*(3), 184–88. Retrieved from http://www.jstor.org/stable/40033175

Graham, S., Gillespie, A., & McKeown, D. (2013). Writing: Importance, development, and instruction. *Reading and Writing, 26*(1), 1–15. http://dx.doi.org/10.1007/s11145-012-9395-2

Graves, D. H. (1994). *A fresh look at writing.* Portsmouth, NH: Heinemann

Luke, A., Sefton-Green, J., Graham, P., Kellner, D., & Ladwig, J. (2018). Digital ethics, political economy and the curriculum: This changes everything. In K. Mills, A. Stornaiuolo., A. Smith, & J. Zacher Pandya (Eds.), *Handbook of writing, literacies, and education in Digital Cultures* (pp. 251–61). New York, NY: Routledge.

Newkirk, T. (1982). Young writers as critical readers. *Language Arts, 59*(5), 451–57. Re-trieved from http://www.jstor.org/stable/41404043

Routman, R. (1991). *Invitations: Changing as teachers and learners, K-12.* Portsmouth, NH: Heinemann.

Stotsky, S. (1983). Research on reading/writing relationships: A synthesis and suggested directions. *Language Arts, 60*(5), 627–42. Retrieved from http://www.jstor.org/stable/41961512

Tompkins, G. E. (2002). Struggling readers are struggling writers too. *Reading & Writing Quarterly, 18*(2),175–93. http://dx.doi.org/10.1080/10573560252808530

Yancey, K. B. (2009). 2008 NCTE presidential address: The impulse to compose and the age of composition. *Research in the Teaching of English, 43*(3), 316–38.

Annotated Bibliography

(Re)Considering Your Teaching Approach to Writing

Gallagher, Kelly
Teaching Adolescent Writers.
Portsmouth, NH: Stenhouse, 2006.

With great humor, Kelly Gallagher shares with readers his approach to teaching adolescents to write well. Gallagher provides examples to emphasize the importance of student choice, mentor texts, and establishing writing as a priority as key to student success. Assessment is considered, but only within the bigger picture of a comprehensive writing approach.

Rief, Linda
Read Write Teach: Choice and Challenge in the Reading–Writing Workshop.
Portsmouth, NH: Heinemann, 2014.

An open invitation to Linda Rief's classroom, *Read Write Teach* provides us with a year of reading and writing approaches to easily implement with adolescent learners. Rief frames her teaching approach with the importance of building a community of readers and writers and holding true to the fundamental belief that all students can be successful readers and writers. As with all of Rief's work, she speaks with authenticity and a lived-it perspective that all teachers can respect and appreciate.

Warner, John
Why They Can't Write: Killing the Five-Paragraph Essay and Other Necessities.
Baltimore, MD: Johns Hopkins University Press, 2018.

John Warner sounds the alarm on what decades of teaching-to-writing formulas and high-stakes writing assessments have done to the writing trajectory of our students. Warner provides a solid framing for what has gone wrong and how we might begin to solve the problems that we—educators, policymakers, and, in part, parents—have caused. A great book study selection, Warner's book puts writing pedagogy under the microscope.

Cultivating the Culture of a Daily Writing Community

Goble, Pam, and Ryan R. Goble
Making Curriculum Pop: Developing Literacies in All Content Areas.
Minneapolis, MN: Free Spirit Publishing and NCTE, 2016.

Cultivating a culture of daily writing can be difficult, especially when students often ask us, "What can I write about?" Goble and Goble's approach to capturing the attention of our students is simple: build a bridge from what students are interested in learning to the skills we want students to acquire. Offering a variety of approaches to reading, writing, listening, speaking, and viewing media, this book helps teachers guide students to think critically about what they've read and to use their work as a springboard for future extended writing projects.

McGregor, Tanny
Ink and Ideas: Sketchnotes for Engagement, Comprehension, and Thinking.
Portsmouth, NH: Heinemann, 2018.

Sometimes daily writing doesn't begin with writing at all. McGregor shares how to harness doodles into sketchnotes, a visual note-taking approach that helps make learning more visible and allows students to record their critical thinking through a variety of think-aloud strategies. The book is full of examples and is applicable to learners of all ages.

Rief, Linda
The Quickwrite Handbook.
Portsmouth, NH: Heinemann, 2018.

Quickwrites are writing to find writing, Rief explains, as she shares the importance of helping students put words on paper. Sharing 100 mentor texts, Rief describes her approach and provides examples to guide teachers in writing and helping students to build stamina and confidence in developing their ideas and writing skills.

Teacher as Writer

Dahl, Karen L.
Teacher as Writer: Entering the Professional Conversation.
Urbana, IL: National Council of Teachers of English, 1992.

One of the first professional books written to situate teachers as active writers in the classroom, *Teacher as Writer* features teacher-writers sharing their stories of "becoming," helps teachers believe in themselves as writers, and guides teachers to share their writing with larger audiences. Tips for developing professional writing, writing groups, and publishing are shared.

Hicks, Troy, Anne Elrod Whitney, James Fredricksen, and Leah Zuidema
Coaching Teacher-Writers: Practical Steps to Nurture Professional Writing.
New York, NY: Teachers College Press, 2017.

This all-star team of teacher-writers shares practical strategies and examples of ways to encourage and lead teachers to be writers. Motivating teachers to write and to share their writing is the first step, with tips for sustaining the practice as a way to better understand their students, their practice, and themselves. Ultimately, the book is grounded on the philosophy that the best teachers of writing are writers themselves.

Kittle, Penny
Write beside Them: Risk, Voice, and Clarity in High School Writing.
Portsmouth, NH: Heinemann, 2008.

Even though the title indicates high school writing as a focus, all of what Kittle shares is applicable to middle level learners. An intimate look into Kittle's decades of teaching experience, the book shares Kittle's approach to planning, writing, and sitting alongside her students in writing conferences, building a relationship of trust that fosters adolescents' willingness to stretch their skills and take chances with their own learning.

Considering the Bigger Picture of Our Classroom Work

Ahmed, Sara K.
Being the Change: Lessons and Strategies to Teach Social Comprehension.
Portsmouth, NH: Heinemann, 2018.

Classrooms are often the first places students have the opportunity to ask about and consider difficult topics. Ahmed provides a social comprehension framework for teachers, with activities and strategies included, to assist students in addressing issues that impact our students and our world. Dealing with social issues in the classroom can be complicated, but Ahmed's suggestions can help cultivate a culture of empathy and open dialogue with adolescents.

Busching, Beverly, and Betty Ann Slesinger
"It's Our World Too": Socially Responsive Learners in Middle School Language Arts.
Urbana, IL: National Council of Teachers of English, 2002.

Busching and Slesinger share their approaches to discussing and studying significant social justice issues with middle level learners. Through a collaborative inquiry approach, adolescents research poverty, race, gender, and other diversity considerations through thoughtful noticing, questioning, and examining what it means to be an active citizen.

Christensen, Linda
Teaching for Joy and Justice: Re-imagining the Language Arts Classroom.
Milwaukee, WI: Rethinking Schools, 2009.

Christensen has long been at the forefront of social justice education. In this text, she shares her experiences of being a learner alongside her students as they consider their own lives and interests as the driving force in their learning journeys. Concrete examples provide the reader with motivation to think critically about empowering adolescents to take control of their learning through choice and expression.

Mirra, Nicole
Educating for Empathy: Literacy Learning and Civic Engagement.
New York, NY: Teachers College Press, 2018.

Through the traditional elements of English language arts such as writing, reading, research, and discussion, Mirra provides a framework for modeling empathy with adolescents to foster critical thinking and to provide mentoring for ways to lead discussions or respond to socially and emotionally charged topics and conversations with care and concern for others.

Digital Resources

National Writing Project
www.nwp.org

Voices from the Middle
http://www2.ncte.org/resources/journals/voices-from-the-middle/

Voices from the Middle podcast
http://www2.ncte.org/resources/journals/voices-from-the-middle/podcasts/

Inspirational Literacy-Related Social Media

#movingwriters
#NCTEVillage
Allison Marchetti @AllisonMarchett
American Library Association @ala
Antero Garcia @anterobot
Assembly for Literature for Adolescents @alanorg
Brian Kelley @RealBrianKelley
Chris Lehman @iChrisLehman
Chad Evertt @chadeverett
Colby Sharp @colbysharp
Donalyn Miller @donalynbooks
Ebony Elizabeth Thomas @Ebonyteach
Jennifer Gonzalez @cultofpedagogy
Jennifer S. Dail @jennifer_s_dail
Kate Roberts @teachkate
Kylene Beers @Kylene Beers
Linda Rief @LindaMRief
Margaret Robbins @WriterMar
National Council of Teachers of English @ncte
National Writing Project @nwp
Penny Kittle @pennykittle
Rebekah O'Dell @RebekahODell1
Sara Ahmed @SaraKAhmed
Sarah Bonner @MrsBonner301
Sara Kajder @skajder
Shanetia Clark @uvagradu8
Tracei Willis @t_writenow
Writers Who Care @writerswhocare

Index

The letter *f* following a page locator denotes a figure.

Editor

Shelbie Witte (@shelbiewitte) is the Chuck and Kim Watson Endowed Chair and Professor of Adolescent Literacy and English Education at Oklahoma State University, where she directs the OSU Writing Project and the Initiative for 21st Century Literacies Research. She serves as editor (with Sara Kajder) of *Voices from the Middle*, NCTE's premiere middle level journal. Witte has published extensively in the area of literacy in a digital age, including coediting *Literacy Engagement through Peritextual Analysis* (2019) with Don Latham and Melissa Gross.

Contributors

Sarah Bonner is a veteran language arts teacher at Heyworth Junior High School in Heyworth, Illinois, as well as a current doctoral candidate in the School of Teaching and Learning at Illinois State University. She has published works in *Middle School Journal*, *Middle Grades Review*, and *Voices from the Middle*, and is the co-creator of TeachWhys. Her work focuses on inquiry-based learning in the middle school classroom. You can learn more by following her on Twitter: @MrsBonner301.

Matthew Homrich-Knieling is a middle school ELA teacher in Detroit, Michigan. He is also a cofounder of MIStudentsDream, a coalition of educators, students, and community members organizing and advocating at the intersection of immigration and education justice. His work has appeared in *Teaching Tolerance*, *Voices from the Middle*, and *Education Week*. His teaching and organizing focus on community-based and culturally sustaining pedagogies, youth organizing, and restorative justice. *The views expressed in his chapter do not necessarily reflect the views of his employer.*

Frances Lin is a middle school ELA teacher in Tracy, California, who also teaches university courses for preservice teacher candidates. She is the current chair of the NCTE Middle Level Section Steering Committee and a member of the NCTE Executive Committee. Lin is a poet and writer with several publications on the teaching of writing and assessment in education. She also specializes in nineteenth- and twentieth-century poetry and in critical theory. She is currently working on multiple writing projects in the creative writing genre.

Joseph S. Pizzo is a 46-year veteran teacher of middle school English at Black River Middle School in Chester, New Jersey, and an adjunct professor of communications at Centenary University. An author and poet published by *Barron's*, NCTE, NJCTE, NJAMLE, *DisruptED TV Magazine*, the NEA Foundation, and the US Office of Veterans Affairs, Pizzo hosts the NCTE *Chatting with Emily* podcast and is the former host of WRNJ's *When the School Bell Rings* and DisruptED TV's *School Spotlight*. An original member of WWOR-TV Channel 9's A+ for Teachers Hall of Fame and the NCTE Historian, Pizzo is a member of the NJ Autism and NJ Education Think Tanks. Follow him on Twitter: @ProfJPizzo.

Margaret A. Robbins teaches middle school humanities at The Mount Vernon School in Atlanta, Georgia. Her work has appeared in the peer edited periodicals *The ALAN Review*, *SIGNAL Journal*, *Gifted Child Today*, *The Qualitative Report*, and *Social Studies Research and Practice*, as well as in the edited academic books *Fantasy Literature: Challenging Genres* and *Comic Connections: Reflecting on Women in Popular Culture*. Robbins's research interests include comics, young adult literature, fandom, popular culture, autoethnography, narrative inquiry, critical pedagogy, feminism, and writing instruction and practices. Learn more about her teaching and writing on Twitter (@writermar), Instagram (@dr.margaretrobbins), and her blog (https://drmargaretrobbins.blogspot.com/).

Tracei Willis is a teacher, voracious reader, writer, and social justice warrior. She has completed more than 300 hours of education in the history of the Holocaust and the Civil Rights Movement. As a teacher trainer for The Olga Lengyel Institute for Holocaust Studies, she plans and directs a three-day seminar each summer in her home state of Mississippi to train educators to teach about these critical topics. Willis never misses an opportunity to put books in the hands of kids of all ages. This year she is teaching fourth grade and feeling the love from her small humans.

Lauren Zucker teaches English language arts at Northern Highlands Regional High School in Allendale, New Jersey, as well as education courses at Fordham University. She serves as editor of *New Jersey English Journal* and co-chair of NCTE's ELATE Commission on Digital Literacies and Teacher Education. Her recent work has appeared in *Reading Research Quarterly*, *English Journal*, and *Contemporary Issues in Technology and Teacher Education*. Read more about her teaching and research at laurenzucker.org.

This book was typeset in Janson Text and BotonBQ by Barbara Frazier.

Typefaces used on the cover include American Typewriter, Frutiger, and Formata.

The book was printed on 50-lb. White Offset paper by Seaway Printing Company, Inc.